A PERIL TO MYSELF AND OTHERS

My quest to become a captain

David Kilmer

For Berto, forever my little sidekick

Life is like stepping onto a boat that is about to sail out to sea and sink.
—Shunryu Suzuki Roshi

A river pilot, in those days, was the only unfettered and entirely independent human being that lived in the earth.
—Mark Twain

INTRODUCTION

If you want to be a sailboat captain, go to the islands. That's the advice I got before I packed my seabag, threw caution to the wind and booked a one-way ticket to an unfamiliar land. I left my other life behind and went all in, abandoning the familiar and welcoming the strange.

That new life was more intriguing, funny, scary and spectacular than I could have imagined. The sea magnified everything. As the bright Caribbean days unfolded, I experienced wonder, fear and longing in ways I never had before.

I spent those seasons with a cast of characters: crazy old salts, young smugglers, A-list movie stars, wealthy guests, black sheep boat bums and beguiling islanders. I wrangled boats through wind, weather and breakdowns. Through it all, I saw the world with a blazing intensity. It was genuine and unforgiving, stunning, powerful, treacherous and quite often insane.

Boats demanded their price for the freedom they delivered. I've never had another job that was so close to the bone. Boats took their bites out of me, literally and figuratively. I was beaten, burned and otherwise humbled by the raw physical nature of the work. And I loved it.

Along the way, I learned the right way to poop on a boat, ways to keep from being seasick and how to keep the boat in one piece and off the reefs. But more than all that, I learned a new way to be in the world. My time as a Caribbean boat captain changed me profoundly.

The way was sometimes dark, sometimes silly and always beautiful. This story is part travelogue, part philosophy, part primer on the business of working in yachting for others who would follow in my footsteps. It's for anyone who has ever jumped headlong into something new or fantasized of doing so. This book is for dreamers and doers, for those who love the thrill of foreign shores and sensations, either in real life or the imagination. And for anyone who's ever taken on a challenge.

Here it is, the secret life of a boat captain in all its adventure, wonder and sometimes misery. At some point in my job, I found myself wanting something bigger and better. I got that, and you'll see how it turned out. Be careful what you wish for, my friend.

I went to the islands to prove myself, and I did. I wanted to squeeze absolutely everything I could out of life, to take the biggest bite imaginable and see how it tasted. I wanted to see, know and feel, and those islands did not disappoint me.

Thank you for hopping aboard. It's an honor to take you along for the ride.

–Capt. David Kilmer

SOUTH

IF THE PATH BE BEAUTIFUL, LET US NOT ASK
WHERE IT LEADS. –ANATOLE FRANCE

As a younger man, I once flew to the Caribbean to chase an unlikely dream of running sailboats for a living. I stepped off that turboprop plane with one bag, very few boat skills and no idea what came next.

That leap was both punished and rewarded in great measure. In the five seasons I worked in St. Vincent and the Grenadines, I found myself way over my head more times than not. The work was frightening, exhausting, hilarious, tragic and absurd. And it was the best thing I've ever done.

In this wayward string of islands, scoured by wind, sun and salt water, I found a life I'd desired without even knowing it. I've never been quite the same.

How does a land-bound kid in Idaho wind up as a captain in the Caribbean?

It really came down, like a lot of life does, to just showing up.

We've all taken those leaps of faith; we take them every day. It's just that some are bigger than others. At the time it was a significant plunge for me to abandon a good job at a ski resort in exchange for a vague faraway promise in an email.

An even bigger dive was getting on a plane for someplace new on the map, leaving everything behind just to see what was out there. It's not easy to start over and design your own life, to swim upstream against the current when everyone else seems headed the other way.

I loved working in the ski business. I appreciated the mountain culture, the tribal aspect of it, certainly the absolute joy to be found riding my snowboard giddily downhill after a foot of new snow. But each low-pressure system, the Pacific storms that dumped fresh powder and should have brought contentment, sent me into a tailspin.

At night I wandered the streets of the little town trying to look up past the clouds to see if there were any stars. By degrees I realized I envied the people who skied our mountain by the season, then left to a different hemisphere to do it all again.

Then I began to have these incredibly vivid dreams about sailing on the ocean, a subject I knew very little about.

I had been to sea just once before, on a small boat across the Pacific with Gartly. He was the first person who ever told me you could live on a boat and take it anywhere you pleased. This was an astounding thought.

He was a dark-eyed pied piper, a serious-minded shaman of music, books and the world. Hanging around Gartly, riding shotgun in his old pickup truck in search of trout, I had the sense that something bold and interesting might come next over life's horizons.

Long odds brought us together at a small private college in the Pacific Northwest outskirts. I was just off the plane from Africa, the faithful son of missionary teachers, while Gartly was cutting classes for California surf breaks and trekking Nepal.

America seemed strange to me on re-entry, and private college was especially puzzling. The other kids were mostly decent, but they seemed quite unaware of the Very Big Thing of which I was just beginning to catch these glimpses: the mystical nature of it all, seen in a woman's faraway eyes, in wild animals and wild places, in backroad trips, rivers, old books, south winds, new dreams, shreds of conversation, lines from a song.

I had an outsider's view of these sharp-dressed boys determined to elbow their way into the lead and those girls in sundresses at hopeless arm's length ("We're just not their ticket out of town," Gartly once said). It all looked a little too tidy to me. They were no doubt bound for the nicer side of the suburbs, their life's trajectories mostly mapped by the time they came of age. I was headed for more uncertain aspirations. I just wanted to feel and know absolutely everything there was.

Gartly took his English degree to the wilds of Alaska, where he put in long shifts on a fish processing boat. In those dark, heaving depths, with machinery rattling perilously around him, his shipmates ex-prisoners slinging blades on the line, he read the classic novels and he thought about a boat.

He made his fish money and he bought that boat, and he sent an intriguing letter I received at the small town newspaper where I worked.

"This is the devil talking... quit your job and come south," the letter said.

I was lured, as countless sailors had been before me, by the promise of open spaces and exotic ports, and above all a chance to see over the horizon and find something new. I took the bait.

My time aboard *Marlin*, Gartly's simple and sturdy Cal-34 sailboat, was a voyage of discovery at every turn, especially for the 21 days we sailed a blue stretch of wide-open Pacific Ocean from Mexico to Hawaii. In those lovely, terrible days of life underway in a vast ocean, I was treated to a front-row ticket to the Big Show itself.

Sun, stars, wind and clouds rolled along on a grand scale. A solitary sea turtle paddled up through the long transparent swell, a thousand miles from land. Brilliant bioluminescence streamed in our night wake. As we performed our chores of eating, sailing and keeping watch by turns, I found that the thundering power of my human emotions rivaled those waves carrying our ship along. By turns, I was swept by fear, exhilaration, doubt, wonder and near-psychosis.

The sea magnified everything. With everything to lose, suspended in the immensity of the universe, the sensations were off the chart. By the time the green volcanoes of Hawaii rose by degrees off the bow and we coasted to the customs dock in Hilo, you might as well have stuck a needle in my arm.

Some people climb off the boat at the end of that trip, kiss the dock and never go back out there. I did kiss the dock but I wanted more of everything we'd found out at sea. Whenever I've experienced one of the highs or lows of sailing since then, I've whispered to myself, or sometimes called Gartly himself to say, "It's all your fault, man."

So in my early 30s, whenever that south wind blew down from my ski mountain, I felt a melancholy tug. We've all felt it and called it by different names. Mine was the vision of a sailboat in a big blue ocean. It was time to go.

And at a time in my life when the odds told me I should definitely be buckling in and settling down, I went the other way.

I gave three months notice to certainty and began packing my seabag for high uncertainty. The destination was a tiny island in the Caribbean where I might have a chance of working for a charter company.

Charters are a way for people to experience an exotic sailing trip without owning a boat themselves. Various companies, usually in the planet's most beautiful places, gather a fleet of boats that can be rented for days at a time. Sometimes those boats come with a captain. This one particular company, in a place I'd never heard of before, might have use for a captain. That was the premise upon which I was essentially starting over with my working life and my place in the world.

It's a powerful thing, abandoning the familiar and welcoming the strange. That departure south was unexpectedly hard to handle. The long plane ride, or series of plane rides, from the Pacific Northwest to the Caribbean gave me plenty of time to think of all the reasons not to go.

With my mind, and my mojo, just as unsettled as the turbulence under the airplane wings, everything I cared about shrank behind me: An incredible woman, my small pile of earthly goods, a few friends and the Northwest mountains and rivers where I felt best. There was a physical agony to the parting.

And yet, somehow I knew I had to do it.

ARRIVAL

BE WHOLLY STILL AND ALONE. THE WORLD WILL PRESENT
ITSELF TO YOU FOR ITS UNMASKING, IT CAN DO NO OTHER.
IT WILL WRITHE IN ECSTASY AT YOUR FEET. –FRANZ KAFKA

Yowser, that first landing was a jolt. All I could see through the mist was sharp green peaks as the plane bounced and yawed in the updrafts and the passengers cried out and prayed. Somehow on the third pass we found the runway.

As I stepped down the stairs, those first impressions were overwhelming. I saw goats along the tarmac and steep, impossibly verdant hillsides. Rain came instantly, hammering red tin roofs and making us all run for cover. The air was dense and hot.

The taxi van driver in his Rasta cap wrestled through the potholes. "Rough seas, mon," he hollered.

He took the corners at speed, the pretty island girl next to me giggling each time we collided. Soca music vibrated the van and pummeled my kidneys. A boy conductor leaned out the door, urging more passengers to wedge inside. With much manic revving and braking, we raced other rigs with their names painted on the back, passing *Easy Rhydah* on a blind mountain curve and

Jah Live in a bold move on the straightaway. Lean dogs and rum shacks whipped past. The driver took pride in each overtaken rival: "We clean up on dat race."

Then he pulled over to chat forever with two gussied-up ladies as the other vans flew by, honking their victory.

It was tropical dark when the van dropped me off. I drank in that rich air, a thousand jungled plants exhaling around me. I reveled in the tree frogs and the strangeness, a moment that only diving into the deep end headfirst could bring. That night was thick with the promise of something. It was all there, waiting for me; a reckoning of things I might gain for all I had just left behind in my other life.

I remember hearing a coconut, dislodged by wind somewhere above my head, crash down right beside me. Was it a warning? Tired, hungry, lonesome and having second and third thoughts, I finally found the place. An open-air bar with a tilting dock and a few lights strung overhead. I'd come so far for this?

The night guard, another Rastafarian, showed me to a boat, heaving in the ocean surge. Weariness finally won against fear and excitement and I slept until rain pounded the deck above my head. I crawled out to check the mooring lines in the squall, naked and drenched. My heart, woken from strange dreams, thumped wildly for a long time.

In the morning I stuck my head through the hatch to find the air was clear and a postcard view lay in every direction around the bay. There were shreds of rainbow, green jungle, pink houses and blue seas.

I was right where I belonged, or was I?

SALT

TREAT EVERY FRENCHMAN AS IF HE WAS THE DEVIL
HIMSELF. –ADMIRAL HORATIO NELSON

I was now a vagrant, unsure of my surroundings and, to be honest, my general purpose in life. I tried to make some order out of the broken sailboat that was now my only home.

The wind was constant here: roaring at night, howling in the day, shrieking in the squalls. With wind driving against ocean, everything was salt. With salt in my hair, my skin and my mouth, I kept to the lean daily rituals to stay sane, took meals at the bar on credit when I got too hungry and waited for life as a captain to somehow arrive.

The sailing charter base looked like an abandoned movie set fading in the sun, the buildings slowly unmooring from the jungle and sliding toward the sea. A fleet of boats came and went, tended by outcasts who lollygagged around the place.

Chief among them was Cookie. Of all the old salts who lived in these in Caribbean backwaters, old Cookie had to take the prize. He smelled like decaying timber and tobacco, and in the afternoons, rum. It was impossible for me to comprehend much of anything he said in his thick Liverpudlian accent, delivered through missing front teeth and a scraggly beard.

There were rumors of a Mrs. Cookie who paid him to stay away, and darker tales that he was banished from his native land for life, perhaps for murder. Someone told us Cookie was an orphan, taught to sail on the Thames by old-timers who'd served in the Merchant Navy when ships still sailed instead of steamed. In this version of his story, those ancient mariners hobbled up and down the banks in odd hats, hollering stern admonitions to young Cookie at the tiller of his tiny craft.

He did have a temper born in the streets and perhaps honed on long, bleak solitary ocean crossings. One morning, another captain came down to breakfast with a tremendous black eye. He waved off any explanations. When Cookie limped into the room, grunting with weight and age, he ignored the other guy, but gave me a vicious wink and held up a fist, middle knuckle protruding.

"Always give 'er a twist, right at the end," he said.

We knew old Cookie had been at sea long enough to survive several hurricanes. He hated fools, Yanks and new recruits, which meant I was out of grace on all counts. So naturally the charter boss decided old Cookie would be my one and only guide to the islands before I was on my own. We boarded a puddle jumper plane together, Cookie making it obvious he was quite annoyed to have an imposter along.

As a bejeweled string of islands rolled dreamlike under the wings, I felt increasing panic. In my mind's eye, I was already running aground in an expensive boat on one of the unmarked reefs below. I begged Cookie for some local knowledge, but he turned his salt-stained brim away, stared out his own window and gave a series of grunts.

I was convinced our plane would crash. We came into that short runway at such a steep angle there was nothing but tarmac filling the windshield. Then came a hard flare and full roaring reverse as soon as the wheels touched down. Cookie didn't flinch.

We forged an uneasy alliance, the Brit and the American, to move a boat northward, a bash against wind and waves. As we made the slow miles, Cookie insisted on one thing: his beloved *Abbey Road* should be played at top volume on the stereo at all times. Whenever he saw a French-flagged vessel go by, he would flick them the back of his hand, fingers V-ed in a reverse peace sign.

"The Agincourt salute," he said, telling me how the French had vowed to chop off the arrow-pulling fingers of his ancestors' longbowmen.

"I've still got me own here, Frenchies."

He was a man of a certain kind of honor and would not drink until the anchor dropped. Then the rum evaporated and he would talk a little in that impenetrable accent of his. Still, most of his secrets remained intact.

Somewhere along the way, I finally scored some points with Cookie when we had one engine go down. Using my Leatherman and a lucky bit of shade-tree mechanics, I got it running again. His bushy eyebrows went up, but he didn't say anything. When the boat's second engine went, and I sweet-talked that one back to life, too, he jerked his chin in appreciation.

"Bloody 'ell."

It was the biggest praise I'd ever get from old Cookie, and I took it to heart.

It seemed we were now friends in the ways boats will do. Still, there had been no briefing on my new workplace. I would have to figure it out as I went along.

TERRORS

DANGER HIDES IN BEAUTY AND BEAUTY
IN DANGER. –BELVA PLAIN

I f I'm quite honest, my strongest sense in those early Caribbean days was dread. Every day I squinted out at the wind-scoured sea beyond my sheltered lagoon and wondered what Thing had my name.

I had barely begun my quest for who-knew-what, and already I was facing the monsters guarding the gates. Warnings came unsolicited from expats and locals alike; at the bar, in the taxi and on the dock, murmured by the security guard in the thick tropical night.

Everyone seemed eager to tell the worst.

"This boat blew up and nobody know why."

"Them people hurt real bad with a cutlass."

"This other fellow got mash up and the ambulance took too long. Anyway, better you die than go to that hospital."

Fear. No other word for it.

Fear from the time I could remember. That faint hum of dread underlying my happiest of childhoods. Fear of failing and being cast out, rejected. Fear that bad people would hurt me and take

18

the people I loved most. Fear the world would end before I even had a girlfriend. Fear that time was passing.

As a young boy on the beach in Greece, I'd watched a water fight between backpacker kids escalate until one kid grabbed a pot of boiling water and threw it on the other. Those screams I remember.

On arrival in Kenya, where my family lived during my teens, our faculty hosts spent the very first dinner telling us in colorful detail all the ways Africa could get you: Bugs, burglars, killer bees, snakes. Someone somebody knew had hit an animal, or maybe a child on the highway, stopped the car to help, and was pummeled to death with rocks by angry villagers. There was plenty of fear to go around.

For some reason I continued to take these jobs on the edge. As a young newspaper reporter in small-town Idaho, I had dutifully logged the myriad ways we can die, the police scanner next to my bed crackling with another shooting in the night or bloody mishap in the woods. The town had a lumber mill, long winters of discontent and plenty of guns.

I got that job because the last editor had skidded his Jeep on the ice and beheaded himself under a logging truck. The house where I lived had a secret marijuana grow operation in the basement that meant five years hard prison time for all of us if we were busted; I went out to work the cops-and-courts beat hoping the police dogs wouldn't smell it on me.

There was a city councilman who had a serial habit of beating his young wives. I checked his records at the courthouse, investigating like the good little reporter I was supposed to be, and after the very next council meeting he walked me outside with a firm hand on my shoulder. After asking how the new job was going, he got right to the point.

"Funny things happen to people up here," he said, smiling and not quite looking me in the eye, mashing the heel of his cowboy boot into the gravel. "Just want to make sure nothing happens to you."

Now once again, here in the tropics, I was treading where I didn't belong. A stranger in a strange land, I kicked myself for this stupid habit of dropping myself into a new place from which there was no retreat. I wanted very badly to turn and run.

"Just be careful," the man at the beach bar whispered through his cigarette smoke, looking over his shoulder all the while.

Word on the island was that U.S. helicopters were coming back any day to spray the ganja farms on the north end of the island with pesticide, as was their habit. A guy with a collared shirt and a tight haircut ("Those crazy baldheads," as the Bob Marley song went) might be mistaken for a DEA agent and just disappear. The big machete, called a cutlass here, was the weapon of choice. There might be a warning, I was told, in which you'd be kneeled down and whacked on the side of the head with the flat side of the cutlass. Or you might get the sharp side instead. I lived those early island days suspended somewhere between awestruck marvel at this newfound beauty and debilitating terror at what might be lurking behind it all.

Why was I doing this? Again and again I was seized with panic, so hard it hurt. But I didn't want to quit before I'd even begun. I'd done that before and I didn't like the feeling.

Here in this windswept archipelago, there wasn't much solace from the black dog that haunted me. The only thing I could do was find an honest cause and hang onto it for dear life. Right now, that was being a captain, whatever that meant.

HIRED

JUMP, AND YOU WILL FIND OUT HOW TO UNFOLD
YOUR WINGS AS YOU FALL. –RAY BRADBURY

I was trying to pass the time in a hammock with a musty paperback, hungry again and low on morale, when the charter base owner beckoned me. Inside her air-conditioned office, she handed me a plane ticket and some local money and scribbled down a boat name.

Just like that, I had my first gig.

"Please bring it back in one piece," she said, not kidding at all.

The boat was down island and needed to be brought north. This looked to be the common route for deliveries. Guests would sail downwind in comfort, leave the boat and fly home. Boat skippers would do the tougher work of going the other direction against the prevailing trade winds.

When stepped onto my very first command, I remember I was intimidated by how much boat there was to handle. Heretofore, I had done some lake sailing on smaller craft, but nothing of this size. There were many more systems here to understand, or in my fearful mindset, more things for me to royally screw up.

I was also surprised by the boat's messy condition. There was no food left on board, as I'd been assured there typically would be. All the batteries were flat and nothing would run.

Regardless, there was no time for messing around, because as I was soon to learn, a delivery is not a cruise for pleasure. It's a point A to point B mentality. Get there in as few hours or days as possible, without breaking the boat or the crew. And patch things together as you go.

So I cast off the mooring and headed out of the anchorage and into unknown territory. There was so much I didn't know then, and it was probably better that way. I was counting on beginner's luck.

I did have a shaggy haired, happy-go-lucky fellow along, a distant family member the charter base owner insisted I bring as my crew. Likely he was there to keep tabs on me, since I was the new guy, but I wasn't turning my back on him, either.

"Don't let that kid near you, he's psychotic," had been old Cookie's whispered warning.

As the islands slid past, and I tried my best to keep us off the unfamiliar and unmarked hazards, my crew grew fidgety. He kept telling me the best ways to avoid the patrol boats (there were none) and how he needed to stop at this one island and meet a friend.

He sang a Jimmy Buffett number, crooning mournfully and with great feeling the lines about smuggling his share of grass and pissing it away so fast. His melodies and his manner became increasingly erratic.

He left me no choice as captain, and so I finally made him open his bag and show me his package of inspiration. It seems my crew had a different mission on this trip than I did. I forced him to throw the drugs over the side while I watched. He grew sullen and weepy by turns and didn't have much to say, or sing, after that.

In my fledgling delivery I made all the rookie mistakes. I anchored in the wrong place and dredged up a tangle of 18th-century jetsam, so that my first real task at sea was hanging upside down off the bow as we rose and fell in six-foot swells, wielding the sharpest knife I could find and hacking away at this mess while the heavy anchor careened into me. This is the glamorous life of a captain, I said to myself, as I would come to mutter many times again. The blood as I bit my own tongue was a sweet and bitter taste of how close this work could come to the bone.

It's the captain's job to clear the boat in and out of countries, so off I went with passports and cash. Smuggler stayed aboard, still sulking. In the tiny customs and immigration office, I filled out the laborious colonial-era forms in carbon copy triplicate. I was quite nervous about not having a work permit. I tried to look innocent while sweat rolled down my face, making telltale triplicate smudges on the paperwork.

I thought I was done until a uniformed figure pointed me to a small room. I was the only one in there with him. I shifted on a hard bench as he looked me over across his metal desk.

"Listen, I must speak to you about something important," the man said. Long pause. My stomach turned and I knew the jig was up.

"We are taking contributions for our church charity," he finally said. "I wonder if you have any money to spare?"

Boy, did I ever! And so I was back on my way. We pushed the boat hard all day without eating anything, the smuggler and I, and by sunset we were crazed with hunger. The guests had left us wet towels, smelly trash and empty bottles, but very little in the way of food.

I found a few spongy potatoes, a can of beans and a wilted onion and cobbled together a stew. I popped up to scan the horizon and when I returned below, the smuggler was stirring the pot. Taking initiative for once! I was happy to see him back in the game.

I was so hungry it was hard to see straight. We fell on the stew with huge eager bites. I might as well have stuck a flamethrower down my throat.

"Ahhgg!" I choked, my eyes streaming. "Why so hot?"

"I put something in for flavor," the smuggler coughed, his own face on fire.

I looked down and there was the evidence, an empty bottle of the combustible local hot sauce. This kid had dumped the whole bottle in while I was busy elsewhere.

There was no way to get that food past our overwhelmed pain receptors, down our burning throats and into our bellies, try as we might. We tossed it overboard, where some fish must have had quite a shock. We carried on, hungrier and more disagreeable than ever as night fell, and sailed in the dark against company policy in order to make landfall on time. It was one of the intriguing contradictions to be found in my newest life.

After 48 hours of pushing, pulling and pep-talking, I managed to park the sailboat right where it belonged, on time and in one piece. There was a reckless joy to the act. My walk up the dock, while wobbly after two days at sea, also had a bit more of a swagger than before.

"Skip!" the Rasta dock guys hailed me, short for skipper. Nothing sounded sweeter.

In my very first trip, I had threaded unfamiliar waters, ridden rough seas, harnessed ingenuity and a little luck. I had held my little floating world together and delivered it safely back where it belonged.

That evening I was king. My throne was the deck of my battered boat at sunset, my kingdom the islands beyond, my banquet a can of soup (without hot sauce!) and an icy Hairoun.

I was back from the wars and I had saved the realm for another day. My palace had the unspeakable luxuries of a lukewarm shower and cleanish sheets.

As my head hit the rough pillow there was just enough time, as I drifted under, to smile at the thought.

I was a captain.

COWBOY

BUY THE TICKET, TAKE THE RIDE. –HUNTER S. THOMPSON

When I woke on my lonesome sailboat, the rush of accomplishment was gone. In its place was a sour taste which could only be called doubt.

With just one trip to my name, I could feel the physical consequences of my newfound trade: in the rope burns on my hands, the strain in my back from hoisting the outboard, in my sun-blasted skin and boat-bruised shins.

The resolve that had sent me here, thousands of miles from home, was equally shot. With no seafarers in my family, all this unreasonable effort made no sense. Or was there something in the DNA compelling me onward, like a pampered Malamute I once lived with who still buried food before any snowfall?

My granddad on one side of the family was a Swedish lumberjack, and my granddad on the other was an Irish bronc rider and sometime gambler. The cowboys and loggers never did get along, and maybe that explained a lot about me.

My father raised things yet higher, finding a calling as a minister and teacher and spending a lifetime giving in selfless ways to the needy world around him. My mom easily matched his dedication and courage in her career as a nurse.

So for brawn, bravery and character, I had already been bested on all counts. As far as brains, I remembered what the cigar-chomping truck driver had said to me as I struggled to push a wheelbarrow of cement up a plank in 115-degree summer heat. (This was after managing to get a private college degree and foolheartedly turning down a couple of proper job offers).

"Your momma always told you to finish school, didn't she?

He had no idea. Construction lackey, wildland firefighter, newspaper reporter and ski resort worker; I had handled all those roles about as clumsily as that load of wet mud.

So here I was, lighting out into new territory again. Could I make it as a cowboy of the sea, wrangling this herd of unruly boats through wind and weather?

Only one way to find out.

CHARTER

WE WERE LEAVING CONFUSION AND NONSENSE
BEHIND AND PERFORMING OUR ONE AND NOBLE
FUNCTION OF THE TIME – MOVE. –JACK KEROUAC

And then it really happened. It was a day like every other in the Caribbean high season; blue skies, tradewinds, flying clouds. One of those bright, untethered days where nothing might occur, or everything.

A group of decked-out people disembarked from taxis and cornered me at the bar where I was taking my breakfast.

"Are you our captain?"

I wanted to look behind me or run screaming away. Instead, I swallowed hard and forced a grin.

"Yep, that's me," I said in my most confident captain voice.

There was a good chance these people knew much more about sailing than I did. Nevertheless, here we were. Game on.

"We'd love to see our boat," they said. There was a general Type A eagerness to proceed.

Down there in the lagoon, I could see the 50-foot sloop we were supposed to take. Our dock crew was fire-brigading in reverse, handing up buckets of water from somewhere inside the boat and dumping seawater over the side. There were a lot of bucket loads. Nobody wants to get on a boat that's already beginning to sink.

I had to think fast.

"Joseph, how about a welcome rum punch or two for my guests," I said, smacking the bar counter. "I'll be right back."

While the barman plied his magic, the dock crew and I spent the next hour bailing out the rest of the seawater, drying the boat and coaxing the bilge pump to work again. Then we gave our guests a proper welcome aboard with big smiles and nary a drop of water in sight. (Later on in the trip, a guest would be puzzled to open a locker and have a couple gallons of seawater come spilling out, the last of the evidence).

Thus began a set of rituals I would soon cherish: Showing the guests around the boat, casting off lines, motoring out through the cut and raising our sails. When we nosed into the trade winds and shut off the engine, the trip had well and truly begun.

Together, eight academians and I set out to find what these islands had in store. By the time we'd finished that very first cantering reach across to the beckoning island of Bequia, we were all hooked.

We woke when we felt like it, took our coffee at leisure, watched the day unfold and did exactly what we wanted. That first trip I took as a charter captain hinted at enormous freedom in store. It was that kind of freedom remembered from being children with all afternoon to explore, of taking off the training wheels and riding anywhere you wanted, of getting in a Huck Finn raft and pushing off into the current, happy to see what would come next around the bend.

By day we sailed those lucid waters, exploring a new island

every afternoon and cooling off with an ocean swim. By night, we watched the sunsets for the fabled green flash and told stories under the shooting stars, feeling the wind work its spell. My new friends were ever so sweet in overlooking all of my inexpert fumblings, and we got on just fine. I will forever be grateful that they were my first victims at sea.

Halfway through, I had an epiphany about this uncommon trade I'd stumbled into. The trick, I saw, was not just in piloting the boat and staying off the shoals. The real job was showmanship. These people expected something special on the ten precious days they'd managed to carve out. They'd been imagining this trip for months or years. It was the picture pinned to the wall that got them through long weeks of regular life. They had signed up for yachting in paradise.

On the other hand, I knew the unfortunate truths of a stormy weather forecast, a strange sound from the engine and a water system that was "finish up," as they said down here.

Just one thing spanned the breach between dream and reality, and that was the captain.

"Yeah, mate, just get the boat around in one piece," I could still hear the voice of a fellow skipper. "Come back with the same number of people, you're done and dusted."

He was half joking but it was also clear that after several seasons of this he'd had too much. He pushed the boats around and that was enough. He'd come to despise the people who paid our way.

I knew it wouldn't be enough for me. Maybe I was so green I needed to prove myself. Maybe I'd quit too many things in life before. This time I was determined to go all in.

But more than that, I was beginning to take a liking to these ridiculous fellow humans I was stuck with on our little ship of fools. In all their annoying, endearing ways, my guests began to draw me out of my self-absorbed nonsense and win over my shallow soul. On a small boat, we lived, laughed and lamented together, and I'll tell you something, it was amazing.

I thought I was teaching them the boat and the islands. Really, they ended up showing me a lot more.

On that last night of my first trip we sat up late, reveling in what we'd tasted together. Way out there under the stars, every-thing superficial blew away with the howling trades. One of the ladies confessed to all of us that she was dying of cancer. A sail-ing trip like this had been her lifelong desire, and now here she was.

It was a shot to the heart. This was where the last wish led. We were doing what mattered most.

That was the essence of the job: the myriad of lives I would cross paths with on boats over the years, the intimate stories I would hear under the sky and how close to truth we would all come.

POOP

T here is a right way, and most definitely a wrong way, to go Number Two on a boat. This was one of the first and most important things I taught my new sailing guests.

There they were, fresh off the plane, ready for the trip of a lifetime. Nothing brought it back to basics like my heartfelt tutorial on how to use the marine toilet, or head. You could see it dawning in their eyes as they understood what was at stake. More than merely where to find a life jacket or how to use a fire extinguisher, this was information that could make or break their voyage.

Anything we put into the boat's mini-sized toilet was pumped overboard into the ocean by thrusting a handle up and down. Whatever came out the other side, the tropical fish tended to gather around for feeding time, offering unforgettable vignettes:

Cute charter-guest wife: (snorkeling unaware next to the

boat) "Babe! Come look at all these fish! What are they eating?"

Surly charter-guest husband: (sound of toilet pumping and pumping) "Give me a minute here. I'm taking a dump."

Then came the moment of discovery by the swimmer, handled better by some than others.

I soon found myself evaluating my guests on very specific terms. Out here, I judged character in different ways than on land. In short, who among these eager sailors was most liable to break the head?

I loved those people who didn't go near it for days. What were they doing with their poop and pee? It didn't matter. Lovely humans.

Other guests, different story. You couldn't keep them away from the head. They'd spend forever in there, then pump like their life depended on it. I cringed with every stroke, knowing that head was a ticking time bomb.

"I've got an iguana in here, captain, and it won't swim away," one guest said. And he was right.

During one memorable week, I once cleared the same plumbing no less than three times, by hand. I started optimistically enough with rubber gloves, but when it came down to it and I was up to my armpit inside the pipes, it didn't matter anymore. I tried to remember if my hepatitis shots were current, and made every effort not to wipe the sweat off my face.

During the final, deepest and most intricate of those unclogging sessions, where I was now stripped down to my shorts with splatters all over my body and the walls, my client called out through the closed bathroom door.

"Hey captain, when are we headed out?"

In boat charters, just like any hospitality gig, there's definitely a front of the house and a back of the house. This was far beyond the back of the house. The whole bathroom was torn apart, shit-splattered and in no shape for client sensibilities.

From my position, lying on the floor, stretching my arm out as far as I possibly could into warm poop and feeling around for that elusive tampon (why was it a tampon again!) with the tips of my unprotected fingers, I called back in a positive tone:

"Yeah... We're going to be right here for a while. Why don't you take the others into town for breakfast."

"Great. Want us to bring you something?"

"Naw.. (digging yet deeper). I'm good."

Yes, you want to avoid being that perpetrator. So what's the right way to take a dump on a sailboat? Allow me to share some hard-earned advice. It may be the most important sailing lesson you'll ever learn.

First, strive for the shore shit when possible. Savvy sailors have an uncanny way of matching their digestive cycles to trips to land, and thus the problem is solved.

Second, if you must, go while underway. When the boat is moving, everything flows unnoticed into the larger stream. Your bathroom sounds and amount of pumping are masked by the waves against the hull. This works fine except in bigger seas, when, as Gartly once said halfway to Hawaii, "It's impossible to hang on with every muscle in your body and relax just that one."

Third, kindly pre-wet the bowl so nothing sticks there.

Fourth, go easy on the TP. That big wad you like to use back home won't go through the narrow plumbing here and will trigger a bad chain of events.

Fifth, for the love of all things, do NOT flush that tampon. Seriously.

Sixth, don't be afraid to use plenty of water to clear things out, sometimes in stages for those bigger jobs.

Seventh, celebrate. Emerge from the head with a sense of victory. A successful poop on a sailboat, with no eruption from back-pressured lines, no door flying open to reveal you in the act to the rest of the crew, no "It-won't-go-down!" panic is worth a fist pump or two.

Once upon a time, there was a lovely guest who had a real fear of bathrooms, let alone one as public and thin-walled as the one on the boat. She also seemed confused about the specific workings, nervously asking for several briefings on the matter.

Finally the time came. It was a fine evening and the boat was anchored out in one of the Caribbean's prettiest places. Everyone was enjoying this unforgettable night. And suddenly she realized it wouldn't wait.

She was away below deck for a long time, and finally came back asking for help, saying the toilet was jammed. On inspection, there was nothing in the bowl.

"Did you use the head?"

"Yes." A tiny nod.

"Did it go down?"

"No."

"Well, where's the poop, then?"

There was a long pause from this refined creature, and then she whispered.

"I didn't want anyone to see it, so I threw it out the window."

And there it is. You can toss it, flush it, hold it in for a while Sooner or later, we all must poop. And doing so on a boat makes us realize our common human predicament.

We all make waste and take up space. Sharing a marine head,

we see that a touch of courtesy, attention to the job at hand and sometimes maybe a strong throwing arm will get us through.

NOVEMBER

I MOVE, THEREFORE I AM. –HARUKI MURAKAMI

Here I stood again, alone on the deck of a boat in the thick Caribbean night, utterly beat up and completely attuned, swimming through a universe of stars.

It was six weeks into my new existence here, and I'd never felt things so purely before. Maybe it was because I was floating between lives, adrift in a land that was colorful, languid, lush and violent. It was the bubbling lilt of island speak, the sudden drenching rain, the casual mayhem, the breakdowns, the ebb and flow of this place that grabbed hold and would not let you go.

I'd walk past a woman sweeping her dirt floor, pure grace in motion. For an instant as I passed, imagination flared. There are other realities than the one you are born into. In some other life, it might be my house and those were my beautiful kids, and I would come home from the sea, sit down to eat curried fish and tickle the baby's tummy until it giggled.

On nights like this, my body humming with the wind, I could

see in every direction and feel every possibility. I knew I could do anything if I could just figure out what it was. Maybe I would catch a ride on a fast boat to the Med. Maybe I would leave the sea, work the land, marry my love and buy her a horse.

There was a price for all this intensity, to be sure. You had to show up, to face what came at you on both feet and solve whatever came your way. You got here through reading vivid constellations, swimming through flashing schools of fish and climbing a still-smoking volcano. Using your hands, your wonderful reliable hands, to do things you had no idea they could do: fix a diesel, steer a course or rescue another human.

Life here was bigger yet also simpler than it was at home; there was an eloquent contrast in sun and shadow, storms and calm. the windward side and the leeward side. Here, terror, desire and exhilaration flourished in a way not possible back in the real world. Or perhaps this was the real world now, and that other one would be forever unreal.

Yesterday I'd sailed to Mustique, a mind-blowing playground for the jet set, with beaches like powdered sugar and turquoise bays. There lived an enchantress six feet tall, impeccable, her hair twisted up in rows.

"How lahng are you in Mustique?" she said to me. "I only has my teddy bears fah company and I'm gettin' lonely."

She wiggled her inch-long nails and laughed.

"Dese hands cahn do some interestin' tings, ya know."

I had no doubt she was right, but I sailed away before the sirens could lure this voyager onto the rocks.

38

BITES

PENETRATING SO MANY SECRETS,
WE CEASE TO BELIEVE IN THE UNKNOWABLE.
BUT THERE IT SITS NEVERTHELESS,
CALMLY LICKING ITS CHOPS. –H.L. MENCKEN

Yes, as people always ask, there are pirates at sea. Yes, sharks can bite. But the greatest danger to ourselves is always us, and not long into my stint as a charter captain I was proving exactly that.

There were plenty of nicks, scratches and strains. We came to call them boat bites and they were part of the job. But with the constant physical motion and an infinite set of variables, there was always a new way to get good and hurt.

One night I set off a 1,600-degree flare in my fist. It was operator error to be sure; I had pulled it away from a guest so I could demonstrate a safer operation and I was hanging onto the wrong end when I hit the igniter. "Take care to keep the burning end well away from your body," the label says.

Good advice. It was like holding the wrong end of a gigantic match.

My hand reflexively dropped the flare, and I watched it spiraling down into the water with the phosphate still flaming. I knew this one was going to hurt.

"Get me a bag of ice," I told my guests, who were all looking at me with horror.

The island clinic was closed so I was my own doctor. As the night went on, I soaked my hand in ice water until I couldn't feel it, then pulled it out again for as long as I could stand the heat. I self-administered a cocktail of painkillers, trying to work out a dosage that wouldn't kill me.

I sailed the rest of that trip with a gauze-wrapped right hand. Two of my fingers were fused together but did come unstuck. The bandage was a reminder of my folly, and I never made that mistake again.

One delivery job came my way after the previous captain had mangled one finger and lost another in the anchor windlass, his price for distraction at just the wrong time. The blood was still spattered up there when I went to haul anchor myself. It was a lesson in paying attention when it mattered most.

I can caution others because I'm Exhibit A. I've driven a rusted fish hook into the back of my own hand (and had to cut it back out again). The tip of one finger will always be gnarled from that time I trapped it in a block.

I've been caught by the mainsheet and flipped onto a teak deck with a brutality my grandad the bronc rider would have appreciated. "If you're going to be dumb, you better be tough," the other lads admonished.

I've poked my eye and nearly lost it to infection while anchored in the jungle. I've jumped into the water to save a small dog and watched my boat sail away from me, at surprising speed. In short, I have been a peril to myself and others in all the ways you might expect, and some you wouldn't.

But that first season in the Grenadines, the jaws of violence nearly got me in a way that still gives me the shivers.

It was the very last moments of a private charter with well-off clients, a high-ranked member of the European Parliment and his wife. He was determined to learn how to dock the boat stern-to, or Med moor, a sometimes tricky business. My parliamentarian was super nervous about the maneuver and changed his mind twice, but finally went for it anyway.

Into the marina we came. Everything looked okay. We backed toward the docks in slow reverse, boats on all sides, him at the helm and me beside him coaching. As was my habit, I kept my hand near the throttle, just in case.

One of the dock guys beckoned for a line and the wife threw it. The line went in the water and straight for the prop.

"Stop the boat!" I yelled at the politican, anticipating he would use a burst of forward thrust as we had practiced dozens of times. I hung over the back of the boat, determined to grab that errant dockline before it ruined our day.

"SKIP!" Someone screamed.

I raised my head and the concrete dock was coming at me, very fast.

We were so close I actually jumped up onto the dock to avoid the collision, which was hard enough to shake the dock, send fiberglass splintering from the boat and bring everyone running. The guy had thrown it the wrong way into full-speed reverse.

A moment or two later and I would have been crushed between the boat and the concrete pier. If it didn't kill me outright, it would have meant blunt force trauma to the head and chest, on an island with a primitive hospital and no medivac.

Very bad.

I was wrong when I left that throttle and wrong again when I looked away from the action and put myself in harm's way.

It was right that my new friends on the dock were alert, that they shouted, and that I used my natural-born reflexes and jumped with everything I had to save my one precious life.

SPARKS

THE GREAT ART OF LIFE IS SENSATION, TO FEEL
THAT WE EXIST, EVEN IN PAIN. –LORD BYRON

As my first season in the islands went on, my body hardened to the task. My Scandinavian skin browned as best it could. Despite the danger and the physical beating, or maybe because of it, my senses went nuts.

I suddenly had the hots for it all. The velvet air and midnight swims, the foreign chatter on the waterfront, the island girls "walking like a rope unwinding," as Capote wrote. I felt everything channeled through my senses, a giant buzz that would not quit. Going days without a shirt, I was ecstatic at the direct sensual pleasures of sun, wind and motion.

In my first monkish days, a stewardess came off one of the charter yachts and walked up our dock. Those big boats out there were a mythical world, far beyond our lowbrow labors at the front lines. She wore a small sundress, and I'd been living in a ski town where everyone was bundled to the eyes.

I just about fell to my knees with the roll of her hips and a few faint molecules of sweat and perfume that came my way. I could see the dock guys squaring their shoulders, trying to look bigger. As she passed, the wind blew her hair off the white curve of her neck. She picked somewhere to smile, and it was at me. That smile made my day. My next heroic act at sea was for that boat babe, with her long gone and blissfully unaware.

In those islands, even a haircut could be hopelessly erotic. I would walk up a path to sit in a chair in the French wife's kitchen, and while the hot breeze came through the red shutters, she would straddle me, taking her time with the job and murmuring in French as she went. Those haircuts, more than anything, may have ruined me for life. I was annoyed but also grateful for the interruptions from her kids and dogs, breaking the spell.

There was a Danish guest's tall daughter, who matched her lipstick to her new bikini every day and delighted in sun tanning on the aft deck right next to where I drove the boat. As the week went on, and she grew browner, stretching out with a sigh in increasingly skimpier suits, I would have done anything for her and she knew it. Our clandestine affair consisted only of me sneaking her off in the tender to town for cigarettes, a habit I despised but there you go.

We felt this expectant drama about it all; the arrivals, departures and possibilities, the tight quarters and close contact, heightened by the elements, the music and sometimes the rum. Sharing a small craft in these islands had an urgency and abandon. We were all on a brief, burning ride that couldn't last. Stray current sizzled between us wayfarers, who were out here throwing caution to the wind anyway. We were all lost and found in the mindlessness of the moment.

I knew I had already met my one spectacular true love, and I was not down here looking for romance. But I was astounded by the raw energy of attraction this far south. Danger, High Voltage, the sign should have read. Absolutely mesmerizing, but you dared not get tangled up in the wires. The trick was in trying to use all that voltage to do something right, to burn brighter but not to be electrocuted. That beguiling tingle at full power would certainly destroy.

And those French girls!

I was trying my best to teach navigation class to some engineers straight off the plane from mid-winter Chicago. There we sat, six guys crowded in our little cockpit, when a catamaran filled with naked French women and one little French guy pulled up very close. The French seemed to enjoy anchoring right on you, something I would normally protest, but I was helpless here.

Those crazy girls began doing what appeared to be their morning exercise routine, with much huffing and puffing and leaping around.

I tried to keep the focus, but I finally broke down when I looked up to see one girl right next to us doing sit-ups, the other one holding her ankles and counting out the reps in throaty French. Next they all commenced to showering each other on the back of their yacht, laughing in our direction.

Class dismissed. Those engineers would never be the same. They didn't stand a chance of learning navigation that day, or really for the rest of the trip.

Watch out, my friend. Those islands will tease you, please you, take you any which way they can.

They surely had their way with me.

HARRISON

NEVER TELL ME THE ODDS! –HAN SOLO

The day I met Harrison Ford started early. I left St. George's Harbor, Grenada, at first light, gliding past anchored boats under the mountains. I was on my own for this trip. It was high season and we were humping boats as fast as we could, often shorthanded.

All morning I pushed the boat north, taking the fastest route, making good time in the island lees and riding the bucking bronco over big swells off the windward points.

My captain brain was already thinking about customs. One of the dots I had to connect today was clearing the boat, and myself, out of one small island nation and into another. The process was formal and the paperwork hailed from another era (how many dead bodies on board, how many pigs and goats, how many cases of the plague).

Other skippers were annoyed at the time and effort it took; I understood it as a result of the British and French empires' endless colonial jousting here. But I got the jitters whenever I approached. For one, I was laboring here without a work permit, in clear violation of the rules which were marked right on the entry visa. The same uniformed officers were beginning to see my face a little too often, I thought.

The other reason was that when I was around age twelve, my parents, brother and sister and I were detained at the border between Turkey and Jordan in an apparent misunderstanding or worse, and locked in a grim police barracks with no idea when we might get free. Handing my passport to someone in uniform still made me sweat.

As afternoon approached, I sailed through a flock of pelicans fishing inside a rain shower, diving into the sea all around my boat with rainbows flashing off their wings. It was one of those sudden and priceless gifts this game could lay at your feet anytime.

I went past a sweet-looking motor yacht and as close as I could get to shore, lowering my anchor and chain by hand since the anchor windlass was inexplicably "finish up." I rowed the dinghy to the dock and stepped into a classic watercolor town. The customs office was closed and a captain with a briefcase waited outside, smoking a cigar.

"It'll be a while," he said. "They've gone to the other side."

I had a flash of impatience. I could see all my early morning work, my good routing and hard miles, going backward by the minute. In a place where the pace was languorous, and sailboats moved so slowly against the wind and current, I felt like I was always racing the clock; pushing through mechanical failures and weather, and now officialdom, to beat the sudden dark, beat the ferry schedule, beat the plane departure. I was a skipper in constant motion, about as far as could be from the relaxation we promised in our brochures.

The contrast between the other captain and I was unbeatable. He was dressed in sharp-creased whites, gold braid at his shoulders and a hat to match. His gunmetal briefcase gleamed.

I laughed when I looked down at my own ensemble. My surf shorts were crusty with salt and stained with engine oil and blood. I could smell the labors of getting here this morning on my skin, beneath my hastily donned "cleanest dirty shirt," as Johnny Cash sang. There were rust streaks on my arms from the anchor chain and my big toe was bleeding again.

He was one of the first proper yacht captains I'd come across, and I tried not to pepper him with questions. The big boat game was much on our minds in those days, a subject of mystery and envy.

As we waited, two other men walked up to our circle. I guessed they were his yacht crew, matched in tan shorts and logoed caps. They joined our conversation about boats, planes and fish. When one of the men spoke, the voice was unmistakable. There was Han Solo blasting his way back to the Millennium Falcon and Indiana Jones saving Karen Allen from the Nazis. The man all of us boys wanted to be.

I saw the famous grin under his aviators, the scar on his chin. I stuck out my hand.

"Dave," I said.

"Harrison," he said to my delight. "Pleased to meet you."

We all talked for a few more minutes, and then Harrison excused himself.

"Well, I'm going to go find a beer." He walked off around the corner.

The captain motioned me ahead as customs unlocked their office. What I wanted to do was run around the corner after Harrison and offer to buy that beer in exchange for a few more stories. Instead, with the mission still firmly in mind, I cleared out and headed back to the sailboat.

I was pulling up the anchor, hand over hand, when a sleek runabout left the dock, made a hard turn and came my way at speed. When it pulled up, Harrison was driving, which only added to his charm, with most VIPs content merely to ride in the back. Not Harrison Ford!

He pulled alongside.

"Need a hand?" Harrison said.

I spoke way too quickly. Eye-to-eye with the hero, I tried not to sound out of breath.

"I got it," I said. "Thank you."

"OK," he said, and gave me a half salute. "Have a great trip, Dave."

Incredible.

I waved in return, stowed the anchor and set out across the channel as Harrison zoomed into the distance. Already I regretted my hasty words.

"Yes, please," I hollered at myself in frustration. "Grab the helm and let's sail this baby to the next island."

I think he just might have done it, too.

So Harrison, from that salt-stained skipper you treated with kindness at Carriacou, if the offer still stands, you bet, I'd love a hand.

SEABAG

Packing my bag before the next boat trip in those days had a distinctly voodoo vibe. As I placed the simple talismans inside, I hoped they would guard me against hazards, give me comfort and sustenance on the journey and help guide me safely home. When you don't really know what you're doing, or what's about to come your way, those small comforts make a difference.

That routine of packing helped steady the nerves. I found it was a small act within my control, a simple intention. Packing was a way of proving to myself that something only seen on a nautical chart or in my head would hopefully soon be mine.

On a boat, I might live out of that bag for weeks at a time. My first seabag wasn't much: a cheap blue canvas duffel with some bright-yellow rain gear, a battered Leatherman tool and a notebook for writing down the wild thoughts in my skipper's head.

Sadly enough, that first bag had an inglorious end. At the end of a particularly troublesome boat delivery, someone tucked some food into the bag, including a few boxes of long-life milk. I think they were looking at my scrawny frame and trying to feed me. Another well-meaning person, the woman behind the LIAT airline counter, checked my bag and took it away. I would not see it again for nearly a week. "Luggage in Any Terminal," people always renamed the airline, or "Leaves Island Any Time!"

When I did recover my ill-fated bag, it was quarantined to a hot concrete room on the far side of the small airport, where I found it surrounded by flies and the supreme stench of rancid milk in the tropical sun.

It was an odor beyond belief. I went into the men's room to rinse my hands, and there was a LIAT pilot. He took one sniff of me and said, "So you're the guy with the bag." I was infamous.

I had to toss out the bag but I needed that rain gear. I scrubbed and scrubbed, but every time it rained on those foulies, the smell came right back. I finally upgraded my gear and passed the old yellow ones on to Gartly, who now runs his own boat in Homer, Alaska.

For some time after, when it rained, he reported there was still the distinct sour smell of Caribbean long-life milk.

OVERBOARD

There came a day that one of our charter boats sailed itself into the lee of the big island with nobody on board, a proper Caribbean mystery. Two days earlier, one of our fellow delivery skippers, a capable local guy nicknamed Viper, had last been seen picking up the boat down island, sailing solo.

Foul play was always a possibility around here, but it seems Viper didn't have any enemies. Instead, from the looks of things on the boat, a fishing line in the water, a missing gaff, it looked like he had reached out for a fish and simply fallen into the ocean while the boat was under sail. Evidently his crew had bailed at the last minute, and because Viper needed the money, he took the delivery anyway. He was always known for catching fish underway to supplement his meager income.

Going overboard, especially while solo, was something we always knew could happen and now the horror was real. In the warm water, along with the constant drift of the westbound wind and equatorial current, we knew Viper would have had a very long time to think about his misstep as he drifted, slowly but with an awful predictability, over the horizon and away from all the usual routes where he might be seen and rescued.

It was impossible to stop thinking about it. Imagining that tiniest of slips, the empty handed grab for the boat, for something, anything, the water closing over your head, bobbing back up for a breath of air, watching your boat so balanced and beautiful, sailing away from you.

Maybe you would try to swim after the boat, a futile effort, no way to close the distance, just wearing yourself out and the waves breaking over your head. Then wildly swiveling your head around to look for other boats. Nothing there but water, so long your ally and now a treacherous enemy.

Disbelief. Then anger, at yourself, at stupid boats, at the sea. Then the stories you'd heard of sharks. Then a weariness beginning in your limbs as you paddled against the wind. Then drifting, and if you lasted that long, seeing overhead the last sunset you would ever see in your life, and stars that stared down at you so coldly. Salt in your eyes from the ocean and from your tears. Saying your goodbyes to the few people who would ever care or miss you. Then just drifting, drifting, drifting...

I knew firsthand the power of these ocean currents. Anchored off of the private island of Petit St. Vincent, where water runs fast between islands, I'd had three guests jump overboard into those inviting aquamarine depths before I could issue a warning. I was shocked at how quickly they moved away. My tender was still stowed, and swimming after them all would have been futile. I yelled my head off until another boat downcurrent scrambled to pick up my guests. Otherwise they were headed out to sea.

After Viper disappeared, I wish I could tell you the other skippers and I took better safety measures, but I don't think we really did. I guess it was something like the early fighter jet test pilots in *The Right Stuff*. It was easier for us to place quiet blame on poor Viper himself and some small perceived mistake than to admit that we were each one of us capable of drifting over that same horizon.

The nightmare scenario of falling overboard took on a dark but amusing tone in a he-said, she-said account published in the island newspaper.

This American couple had been in a mid-channel crossing when he said she fell tragically over the side. He claimed he tried several distraught attempts to save her, and then unable to raise the alarm and having a hard time seeing through his tears, turned the boat to find help.

She said her husband sent her on deck to do some tricky bit of work, and then something hit her from behind and pushed her overboard. She said her husband made one pass, saying something to the effect of "Rot in hell you so-and-so," and then he sailed away.

Had he checked the local conditions at the time, he might have seen that a rare current was pushing her toward the land instead of away. And had he paid a little more attention to her life story, he would have known that she was a first-rate championship swimmer in high school.

At any rate, when he arrived at his next port of call, there was his wife standing on the end of the dock with her arms folded, a huge police constable on either side of her. What a reunion that must have been!

Last I heard he was still in the local prison, with plenty of time to think about that time he botched the perfect crime of murder at sea.

SEASICK

FACING IT, ALWAYS FACING IT. THAT'S THE WAY
TO GET THROUGH. –JOSEPH CONRAD

One of my happier discoveries at my new job was that I didn't get ill from the motion of the sea. It wasn't the same for all my guests.

One early trip, I couldn't figure out why my liveaboard sailing students were so dull at their lessons. I felt like I was teaching the same class anew each day to a bunch of really nice simpletons; smiling, attentive, but with zero recall, nodding along with their little patches behind their ears. I finally read the label and learned that short-term memory loss is one of the side effects of that patch.

During a week of high winds, I saw we were in for a rough day of bashing north. I briefed the guests to help them keep from getting sick. One lady seemed especially nervous and ate ravenously to combat those nerves, devouring handfuls of her favorite snacks at hand: baby carrots and Pringles.

Once underway, I had my head down in the bilge fixing something (again), and it was rough enough that I was even starting to feel it myself. I had what felt like a bad tension headache from the uncomfortable motion, close work and diesel smell.

"Captain Dave!?" came the call.

The yell was loud and urgent enough I thought someone had fallen over the side. I went sprinting up the stairs to save the day and I fell down very hard in a cockpit filled with acrid goo, an orange jelly of half-digested Pringles and carrot sticks. Our next boat briefing was about how you should always vomit downwind, away from the boat.

Like a lot of things at sea, *mal de mer* is a mystery. We don't know exactly why it happens, what its purpose in our human development might have been or why some of us get it and some don't. Greek history shows those early sailors were no more immune. As long as humans have taken to the sea, it seems we've paid for it by throwing our lunch back overboard.

Even Admiral Horatio Nelson, famed commander of the *HMS Victory,* said, "I am ill every time it blows hard and nothing but my enthusiastic love for the profession keeps me one hour at sea." Charles Darwin wrote to his father: "The misery I endured from sea-sickness is far far beyond what I ever guessed at. If it was not for sea-sickness, the whole world would be sailors."

I found that if my charter guests were miserable, nothing else about that day and that trip mattered, so solving the problem was essential. The normal scenario was moderate nausea the first day or two, which then faded away. Ginger really worked to calm the symptoms. So did those acupressure points on the wrist. Drugs were good for some but had their side effects.

The best plan was making the first few passages short, keeping everyone hydrated and having the potentially ill person stay up in the fresh air and take an active role driving the boat with their eyes on the horizon. The natural ways are often the best.

But nothing on my trips beat one stunning eruption I witnessed in all its glory. I was outbound on the island ferry, which could be a wet and wild ride, especially when the Christmas winds of December and January blew hard.

A local girl climbed to the top deck and sat down across from me, lithe and lovely, wearing a sparkly dress with her hair done up right. She touched her hair and neck, making a striking profile. An island boy sat down to chat her up.

I watched as she told him off, but he gamely stayed with his pursuit as we left the harbor and the boat began to buck. She grew quiet and he leaned in closer, making his best play.

There was no warning at all, just a raw gush of vomit from the glamour girl that absolutely covered young Romeo. He jumped up yelping, pulled off his shirt and flung it overboard. She wiped her mouth, turned the other way, composed herself in an instant and looked every bit as pretty again.

That's one way, I thought, to answer an annoying pick-up line.

Seasickness also worked in reverse. Back on land, taking a long-awaited shore shower, I would feel the entire shower swaying around me. This sensation even had a name from sailors of old: *mal de debarquement,* or land-sickness.

Maybe our bodies just wanted to keep sailing.

HOOKED

WHEN WE REMEMBER THAT WE ARE ALL MAD, THE MYSTERIES
DISAPPEAR AND LIFE STANDS EXPLAINED. –MARK TWAIN

O f all the rituals of my new job, none had greater significance than anchoring the boat. I learned this by waking up one morning, climbing on deck and looking around puzzled to be the only craft in the anchorage.

Last night there were a dozen other sailboats in here, I thought. Where did everybody go?

I rubbed the sleep from my eyes, got my bearings and then spotted our anchorage, a mile away. The other boats were all still there, but we were the ones who had left. In the night, with gusts of wind coming over the hillside, our anchor had dragged slowly and taken us with it.

It was embarrassing for the captain at breakfast, and I took further heat about it the rest of the trip. At least, I pointed out, we'd gone safely out to sea instead of onto the rocks.

At Union Island, I was down below and watched one boat motor forward past us, then another. Why is everybody leaving? Again, we were the ones in motion, dragging backwards. It was time for a fire drill and a humbling lesson in perspective.

I got tired of the tenuous holding there at Union Island, and finally spent a morning with a mask and fins, swimming a grid pattern and digging my fingers into the hardpan marl bottom until I found what I was looking for: A soft patch of sand, shallow, small, but serviceable. I stuck my head up and triangulated a position for that coveted sand, and I could still tell you which palm tree to line up with which red roof to get there.

The fun thing about getting the anchor down early was watching the rest of the arrivals show up and have a go at it.

The long-time cruisers, easily spotted by the amount of extra gear hanging all over their boat, had it down pat. It was a drill they had done hundreds of times. The pro-run yachts had radios, plenty of hands on deck and typically textbook technique. The bareboat charters were the most fun to watch; those craft without a captain, or more accurately four or five would-be captains all trying to run the same unfortunate boat.

It got so we could guess nationality by anchoring style. The Brits did it by the numbers, rakishly attired. With naval commands ringing forth, they would back down in smart nautical fashion to secure their berth for the night.

The French, wearing little, would anchor very close without a glance in your direction. Ten or twelve Frenchies would pile into a dinghy, nearly submerging it. Off they'd head to the bar, all smoking cigarettes as they went, with nary a glance backward to see if the boat still held.

The Italians, colorfully attired, would come in at a dead run, kick the anchor over the side while laughing and joking, then break out the bottles of wine.

The Americans wore gift-shop T-shirts and shouted ideas in a Midwest twang, making a reasonable and hearty attempt at it.

The German boats were easy to spot. Many of the crew would be up on the bow of the boat (where you only need one) with hefty white bodies in tiny shorts, pointing in various directions and debating at length.

We had a bareboat charter guest who came back to base to complain. "I want a new anchor," he said like an idiot. "This one won't hold worth a damn on the coral."

As a lover of the ocean and self-appointed protector of coral reefs everywhere, I wanted to hit him as hard as I could, using old Cookie's special twist at the end of the punch.

The later in the day, the fewer the options to anchor. Conventions of the sea dictate a fair system of first come, first served. But there would always be at least one boat trying to barge their way into a space a little too tight. Sometimes that boat was me.

When you did find a good spot, you learned to guard it well. The ticket to a good night's sleep wasn't just having your own anchor secure, it was making sure there was nobody else anchored just upwind. If I saw another boat beginning to eyeball the space ahead of me, anchor swinging to signal their ill intent, I would stride to the bow of my own command with my arms folded, staring them down.

"Howdy," I would shout. "The holding's no good there. You want to go right-over-there!"

The anchoring drama would carry on into the afternoon, and sometimes after dark. We would watch spotlights dancing wildly and hear high-pitched hollers and sometimes screams, along with the occasional grinding of one boat into another or just a spectacular near-miss. It's why you don't need TV on a boat, we always said. You can watch this!

We all had our turn, sooner or later. For me it was a sudden midnight thump, looking out my porthole to find another face looking back at me from what had been the empty dark.

Our boats were like two mating dogs, determined to be together despite much pushing and shoving from both sides. People kept yelling at me in a language I couldn't understand, insisting I'd dragged into them.

From the position of the boats, I knew they'd dragged into me.

"Who is the captain?" I kept asking.

I don't think there was one. They finally hauled some guy out of his bunk who spoke English, and he and I sorted it out.

The fun part was, they were all Italians, so that after the tempers had eased and the boats were finally untangled, we had quite a nice party.

NIGHTS

LOVE
IS A RIPE PLUM
GROWING ON A PURPLE TREE.
TASTE IT ONCE
AND THE SPELL OF ITS ENCHANTMENT
WILL NEVER LET YOU BE.

LOVE
IS A BRIGHT STAR
GLOWING IN FAR SOUTHERN SKIES.
LOOK TOO HARD
AND ITS BURNING FLAME
WILL ALWAYS HURT YOUR EYES.

LOVE
IS A HIGH MOUNTAIN
STARK IN A WINDY SKY.
IF YOU
WOULD NEVER LOSE YOUR BREATH
DO NOT CLIMB TOO HIGH.

–LANGSTON HUGHES

There finally came a point in the evening when the guests were calmed down, coddled, placated, medicated and tucked into their berths. It was time for the captain to go up on deck, lie on my back, look at the stars and reflect on things.

My thoughts would always start with an inventory of the trip, the weather and the boat: what we broke and what we needed to make it home. I would plan, play by play, the moves I needed to perform tomorrow to make it all happen.

Then I would consider the things I'd seen that day: Sunrise, clouds, water that changed by the hour. I would crave the incredible woman I missed like crazy.

As the moon rose and fell, and the tide chased it around the planet, I would think about the people I've met, known and loved, shared all the good times with and the bad times too.

At night on the ocean, they felt closer than ever before.

In my mind's eye I reached out to my faraway childhood friends from many countries, perhaps never to be seen again.

I thought about girls, starting way back and across continents and time, those youthful wonders and mutual discoveries. Their attraction and their affections became my faith, my medicine and sometimes my downfall. Because I was always in transit, unsure of everything, women became my one constant truth, my something real. Their incandescence was the sun for a sometimes melancholy lad who didn't really know where the center was anymore.

We were all of us feeling the vertigo, our young lives spinning through time zones and checkpoints, a giddy ride with no certain landing place. Countries, culture and creed shifted seismically, and in the upheaval the only thing to hold onto was each other. We teased, flirted, stole kisses and more. We played at love like children tossing a grenade back and forth for fun.

I want you to know this. Your face, your smile, your whispered words and your touch are indelible, seared far into me, a vital part of who I am today. You have comforted me, many,

many more times than you know. Your mischief, your taunts, your wisdom, your ways and your favorite songs I hold close. You have challenged me, lit a fire under me, gotten me through the worst of times sometimes merely by summoning your name and your vital energy. Thank you for everything, with all of my heart.

For anything you did to me that left a scar, I accept it as a small price to pay for what we shared. Those sudden, violent blows to the heart and the gut were a necessary hazing, a rite of passage on the way.

For every pain I caused in turn, I am profoundly sorry.

There we were, kids, really, just trying to figure it all out, sometimes mystified by the magnetic pull between us.

It began in swimming lessons, backyard forts, backstage at school plays, shy trysts, trading letters through the bars separating the girls from the boys at our foreign boarding school.

How well I remember that motorcycle ride with your head on my shoulder and your arms around me, those fierce first kisses in the cafeteria closet, the way we made out under the hot African sun like our young lives depended on it. And maybe they did.

There were miserable goodbye embraces, heartfelt promises made but never kept, always another airplane to catch and another life to live.

You are the dangerous beauty who enticed me into skipping freshman finals week and running away with you. I don't quite know whether to regret or cherish those lost days, because you would die quite violently not long after.

Then I met you camping in the mountains in winter, thrown together because nobody else wanted us around. We shared a tent against frostbite and loneliness.

I carried you at that concert on my shoulders.

We fooled around on an old couch that smelled like your dogs and I tried my best to please you.

You shoplifted Victoria's Secret so shamelessly, and wore it so well before I tore it off your willing and eager body.

You looked at me in that way and I was a goner.

The thrill of being hunted and consumed.

The heat between me and you.

You lied and I lied. My fist went through the wall. Your tears fell in the dark onto my chest. We kept each other company in misery. There were love notes torn vindictively to shreds.

We always loved the road trips, you and I, using travel as a way to hold off time and pretend to change our circumstance, if only for a little while. We went speeding too fast, hopelessly smitten, wild and adrift. We rode the ferry in the San Juan Islands, babbling poetry and seeking shelter. We drove through farm country with the top down in the springtime, taking corners recklessly through the wheat fields. We headed south. You climbed into my sleeping bag in the sand dunes.

We spent those warm nights on a boat, skin on skin, the universe revolving around us, everything else reduced to this.

And so it goes, the ravings and cravings of a midnight sailor. Enough of that.

Sometimes, as the stars shifted overhead and the boat creaked at anchor, I would drift yet further. I would lay there as a kid with malarial fever in a sweat-soaked bed in the highlands of Kenya, watching the hallucinations come and go, wondering if I would die. Or waiting at the Treetops Hotel, listening to big animals moving in the dark, my young boy's heart nearly bursting with the romance and excitement of it all, wondering what else was out there waiting to be discovered.

By now I would be nearly asleep, with all of these people, these places, these adventures swarming over me. Often they would be with me as I dreamed.

But life is brutiful, as the saying goes, and on the night watch, I knew that, too.

So eventually I had no choice, and I had to paddle in my mind's eye through the fateful reflections of Bowron Lake, a provincial park in British Columbia, surrounded by nothing but water, mountains and sky. On that brilliant September trip, fully immersed in the great natural mechanisms and blissfully cut off from all communications, I'd had my life's finest and most ambitious thoughts about the future; for me, for those I cared about most, for the world. As I'd pulled my canoe onto the bank at trip's end, I felt ten feet tall, as filled with joy as I've ever been. The black dog was nowhere to be found.

The first person I met broke the news to me very gently. I still wouldn't believe him, so he showed me a photo of people jumping out of a burning tower. While I'd had my head in the clouds, the world had changed beyond repair. Airplanes had flown into buildings and nearly 3,000 people had died.

In that bright September moment when I first saw that picture, when we all saw those pictures, the dread and pain of being human rushed right back in again.

Yes, my long-lost friends, my friends in the now and my friends to come, life most certainly is brutiful, and I still think of you. And all of that brutality and beauty, the whole of our haunting and spectacular journey, is felt so much more keenly when you are standing the night watch, alone, under the stars.

PURSUIT

WHEN YOU DO SOMETHING, YOU SHOULD BURN
YOURSELF UP COMPLETELY, LIKE A GOOD BONFIRE,
LEAVING NO TRACE. –SHUNRYU SUZUKI ROSHI

"**N**ever been hashing? Aye, you'll love it. Come on!"

So here I was, lost in the trackless rain forests of Trinidad, sliding down a muddy hill with branches whipping my face. I fell into the stream, splitting open my shin.

"Hasher down!" someone yelled happily.

Already I was bleeding in several places, and the hash had just begun.

I'd come here unsuspectingly, to try this strange thing called hashing, with a guy who'd been a mercenary in Angola and sailed a couple of Whitbread Ocean Races. That should have tipped me off. He'd driven the car into the mountains at rally pace, yelling "Rental!" every time the undercarriage struck a rock.

I noticed everyone else wore running shoes. They pointed at my Chaco river sandals, my toes already squishing in the mud.

"Look, dis man in he slippahs!"

They sang some kind of song and shouted advice to the new guy, of which I remembered two things: Watch out for the big snake, and don't grab the bush with the spikes.

"Hashers off!"

Everybody started forward and I followed, eager for any hint of what to do next. Road turned to trail, then to muddy track through the bush. Hashers hollered in every accent from East Indian to Brit to Trini.

"How you go?"

"On, on!"

"Spread out nah fellas, look sharp."

The path ended. We were looking for signs set earlier by the devious harriers who had passed this way, tossing the occasional handful of shredded paper.

The clues led us through rivers, valleys, jungle and fields. We went straight up and down, pulling vines and roots. Footing was treacherous on slippery rock, deep sucking mud and tall grass with unseen tropical hazards beneath.

Still, I began to feel my pace, trotting along and passing a few others.

But what was this? Everyone stopped, the leaders huddled and the people I had just passed came strolling by again.

"What de hell you people? You jus standin' around so?"

Those infernal harriers had led us into a trap. There lay a dreaded X. End of the line.

"Back back!"

The contradictions to this strange sport were becoming plain. I needed the group, but the group was in my way. We wanted leaders, but lead too far yourself and you'd be sent to the back again. Half the time you were running the wrong way. And the best-looking paths were too good to be true.

On we went, wild hashers wearing mud, tumbling down, yelling and breaking into a run at every chance. My plan in my lightweight footwear had been to hang back and take it easy.

But here I was instead, in pursuit of nothing at top speed. It seemed an apt metaphor for my approach to everything else in life.

It made no sense, but I couldn't stop. I shouldered innocent people aside and took risky shortcuts. My feet were going to hate me tomorrow, but now all I could think of was the hash.

We went uphill and soon I found myself near the front. The lead guy lost the trail. I stumbled past him and became the new leader. The elite pack of hashers, lean and seasoned, were breathing down my neck. Adrenaline sharpened my sight of each new mark.

"On on!" It was my turn to yell.

Now came a steep downhill through the jungle. I picked my lines and slalomed down. It was a thrilling narrow existence of keeping my eye on the mark and staying on my feet. I ran past a giant X and realized it had all been for naught. The pack crashed to a stop and retreated. They tried to console me, the new guy.

"Yea, from firs to de las, dis how it go."

The crazy thing went on all afternoon. We splashed up rivers and jumped fences. I ran at full tilt through a field deep with fresh cow dung. My sandals flung the stuff at the lads running behind me and they fell instantly back.

I burst through people's backyards and under laundry lines. I hurdled a couple of ragged dogs that wanted to bite.

In the dark we climbed one last hill, blowing like racehorses. Village kids cheered us on. And then there were the lights of the

70

clubhouse and a crowd still waiting. Turned out I was the third man in. They still couldn't believe my sandals.

"Look here, is the mahn in de slippers. He mad!"

I was scratched, bloody and besmirched. I was a hasher now, and I still didn't really know what that meant.

There was one more humiliating ritual in store. Post race, the other virgin hashers were all forced to drink beer out of their muddy shoes. The only reason I escaped this hazing was because of those Chacos. There was no way to pour a beer inside.

It seemed I was blissfully saved by inexperience once again.

SQUALL

THERE IS A CRACK IN EVERYTHING. THAT'S HOW
THE LIGHT GETS IN. –LEONARD COHEN

I saw it out of the corner of my eye, a smudge to windward off the starboard bow, a tiny blemish on the clear horizon. As I sailed on, that squall stayed put, showing constant bearing and decreasing range, all the signs of collision. On an otherwise perfect afternoon, this one thing and I seemed headed straight for each other.

I was having a splendid sail. The boat had the bit in her teeth, shaking off the swells and galloping along under full headsail and one reef in the main.

I had dropped off my guests the day before, and now it was the captain's turn, this solo romp where I could do just one thing: sail the boat with not one care in the world, shouting and singing into the wind whenever I felt like it. I toyed with the sail plan and balanced the boat until she steered herself perfectly. A joy and satisfaction like nothing else.

The squall drifted taller and now I could smell and feel it, that cool energy of waterfalls and smoke, with every raw molecule beginning to vibrate. Reluctantly I shortened sail in anticipation of the surge of wind and rain I knew was coming.

As a single handed sailor, one careless slip away from drifting to oblivion on the current, I took the greatest heed and deliberation with each new movement. I felt every muscle and tendon lock into place, the wonder of balance, the tightening and loosening of grip, rough rope and smooth wood, the miracle of motion.

But just this once, the wallop never came. Instead, in this strangest of all squalls, something simply opened and my boat was inside. It was an enormous shimmering space, and I sailed silently in awe through that mysterious big room, hearing voices in the wind, seeing rare colors in the mist and feeling with great precision each warm raindrop that landed on my bare shoulders.

For an untold few seconds or hours I looked directly into the eye of the universe without fear. All the flotsam swirling in my head stood still and took its rightful place. Everything in the world held together as I sailed right through the center of it all.

Then the mists wavered, the sun broke in again and the spell was over. My one true squall let go and left me to travel on alone, flashing rainbows in its wake. I watched it go and waved my thanks.

I raised full sail and steered toward my home island, finding my body moving with a wonderful lightness through the rigging, my hands thrilling to the wheel's pull.

I was clear-headed, rinsed from all nonsense and absolutely alive.

TURTLE

NOTHING GOLD CAN STAY. –ROBERT FROST

Violence is always there, even on a lazy island afternoon. This is the story I'd rather not tell.

I was just off a charter, cash tip in my pocket, waiting for the ferry back. I had that post-trip feeling of having reached the summit. I was wrung out but still wired, blasted by sun and wind, wanting home but not quite ready.

I walked the waterfront, away from the ladies selling half cigarettes (cheaper than a whole one) and offers of a taxi. Even here, nobody understood why the common vices did not entice me, or why I would choose to walk when I didn't have to.

As usual I was drawn by the quieter spaces, past the vegetable market and down to the wharf. Japanese money, the rumor went, had built this dock and fish market as trade for a favorable vote so Japan could keep hunting whales. Always, and now, these islands as a pawn in someone's bigger game.

A few small boys were diving into the bay. It was a hot afternoon and everything was in slow motion. Then something rippled through the scene and I pushed forward to see.

A fishing boat had pulled to the dock. The fisherman wore ragged shorts, his torso sculpted by pulling on oars all his life. His face squinted from the constant sun. There were scars on his hands and arms.

More men pressed in to watch as he dumped his catch: a few tired snappers still moving and a small barracuda. His boat was ordinary, built by hand on the beach, paint peeling, powered by an ancient Johnson outboard.

I still didn't understand why we were watching. Here was just another fisherman who slept on the beach, set out into the squally dawn, battered his body against the swell and got whatever slim pickings were left of the fish out there. Maybe he made just enough to pay for fuel again one more day. There were guys like him all over the world.

The protein he brought to the docks through raw physical effort was what kept the island alive. His people could not exist on the starches of breadfruit and arrowroot alone. As Bob Marley sang, "Dem belly full but we hungry... A rain a-fall but the dirt, it tough, a pot a-cook but the food no 'nough."

The fisherman bent into the boat and grunted with effort, his arms lean muscle, tendon and bone. A strange cry went up from the men. It was something between a reverent doxology in church, a lustful groan and the expectant sound before a fight.

I pushed through and there was the sea turtle. She was enormous, the size of a child's wading pool. She had been placed on her back so we saw her underbelly. Her flippers were pierced through and bound together. Her head moved slowly back and forth, her large eyes trying to get a look at us.

To her we were upside down faces, one white and many black ones; the boys dripping wet and crawling to the front, old men, roustabouts, a gangly Rasta with a beard. All of us were in a circle looking at her.

This creature so recently in the sea, and for how many years, how many miles? What far splendors had she seen? Moving with tides, swimming through the huge dark spaces, she was the ocean itself come to life. Turtle and men, we contemplated each other for a moment.

But nothing stays the same.

The turtle's bondage suggested she was upside down in front of us for a reason. New to these islands, I was slow to catch on. The fisherman sharpened a knife as the crowd swelled and the murmurs became more excited. There's a tribal ritual to a feast, the joy of survival together. We Westerners taste it at Thanksgiving. The world feels it each in their own ways, and always around food. We eat, we survive another day, life goes on.

The fisherman carved his initials into the undershell. The turtle looked back at us, calm now. She knew before I knew.

How to tell the rest? I saw the machete appear and then I cried out. I begged to stop this madness, or maybe I only cry out in my nightmares of it. Fumbling hundreds of dollars in tip money from my pockets and stumbling forward.

"How much? How much?" Just another dumb white kid, thinking everything must have its price. So I would buy this turtle and then what?

The fisherman just looked at me and shook his head.

He placed the machete against her belly, hit it with a hammer and split the turtle spectacularly from one end to the other. A bright spatter of her blood came onto us all. Rich intestines welled up. There was a ripple of eager chatter from the men.

The turtle's eyes were bright, her head shaking off the pain, her forelimbs trying to swim away from her own broken madness. It annoyed the fisherman and so he finally slit her throat with the knife. Her head fell back and her blood ran out. Hands reached in to grab slippery hold so the fisherman could begin taking her limbs, twisting until the pop of dislocation. Many hands were now rending at this body. A still-living thing, disassembled forever with no way back.

The thing I can't forget was her breathing. With that turtle torn to pieces, her incredible lungs kept moving. Breath still came and went from the gash in her throat. Every one of those long, hoarse breaths she made was the essence of life. The breaths we all made around her.

That life hung on as long as it possibly could.

That life that fed a village.

That life I still mourn.

TURBULENCE

SUCH A PRICE
THE GODS EXACT FOR SONG;
TO BECOME WHAT WE SING. –MATTHEW ARNOLD

After only one season at sea, airplanes began annoying me. Brash younger cousins to boats, these masters of the air seemed to hold all the cards and call all the shots, swooping down at will to do whatever they pleased. Airplanes cruised in that enviable third dimension, soaring over our daily toil any way they pleased.

I had studied as a pilot before I discovered boats. I knew something of their ways. Navigating the skies held much in common with the seas, but to me, operating those levers and linkages in the confines of a cockpit had never felt like flying nearly as much as the first time I unfurled sails to the wind.

But now those mighty airplanes were taunting me. They were so much more nimble than we were. If I was broken down, adrift, the spare part I needed could have been on that plane. When these sailboats seemed impossibly slow, bucking miserably upwind, those planes overhead were rockets of fleeting derision, winking rudely as they went. Their contrails and their running lights were enough to make me shake my fist at the sky.

The cargo cults of the South Pacific might have had it right after all; those odd silver birds ran the world. It seemed they could bend time and distance at their will while we floated here at the mercy of the elements.

Sure, boats had more glamor, but airplanes always had the last say. Airplanes brought people and they took people away, sometimes rending our hearts with the parting.

Their blinking lights were strange stars, appearing and vanishing above in ways we didn't understand. They were the great deus ex machina, rude overlords, minor gods with capricious whims and uncaring ways. They were the wheels of fate, always grinding, and they made us feel very small.

SPEED

TO ACHIEVE ANYTHING IN THIS GAME YOU MUST BE PREPARED
TO DABBLE IN THE BOUNDARY OF DISASTER.
–STERLING MOSS

If you ever feel like ruining your charter skipper's day, here's just the cheeky little line you need.

First, look back over your shoulder a time or three. Then say, in a tone of mild concern, "Hey captain, does it look like that boat's gaining on us?"

Your captain might feign indifference at first. But observe. First their eyes will stray toward the offending boat. Next, their head will begin to turn from time to time. They will grow increasingly twitchy. A hand may shoot out to tweak something or other. They may mutter about the full tanks onboard, the one time you will hear a skipper complain about having too much water.

Then, finally, they won't be able to stand it anymore, and they'll grab the wheel from whoever is dawdling around there.

"How about a little sail trim," they will bark out, still without acknowledgement of the other craft.

You have cast a cloud over their otherwise sunny existence. And as that other craft draws ever nearer, the captain's mood will continue to darken. You have now inflamed that great passion of the sea, the yacht race.

It goes way back. You can almost picture two of our ancestors, each sitting on their own floating log, holding up animal pelts to the breeze and hooting and hollering at each other in a sailor's taunt even before the language existed.

It is entirely true, as they say, that if two boats are on the same body of water, it's a race. Your boat might be smaller, more heavily burdened or indifferently crewed. That does not matter one bit. The sight of a sail growing larger, creeping into the peripheral vision, then undeniably AHEAD is unpleasant in a way that's hard to describe. To make it worse, the other boat may make a slick and showy maneuver, or simply sail over near you and wave. It just rubs you the wrong way.

So sooner or later, that sort of behavior leads to a sanctioned race itself, and in the Grenadines that race would be the Bequia Easter Regatta.

This is the right island for a boat race. The locals have been building boats here for generations, aided and abetted by the whalers who came here from New England and sometimes never left. The double-enders are lovely little craft that are notoriously difficult to sail. Anyone who wins the Round Bequia race in one of those double-enders has cause for bragging rights the rest of the year. These wooden craft are launched off the beach and loaded with stones and sand for ballast, their gaff rigged sails crackling in the wind along with taunts of courage and conquest, island pride always on the line.

"What bwoy? You bettah know ya onions today!"

"Doan mattah. Ya boat slow as molasses."

"You jus' watch us fly, mistah."

I know a man who built such a boat on the beach in front of his house. He and his four brothers drew lines in the sand instead of making a blueprint. Then they set out into the island scrub to find timber. In an elegant solution that turns Western design and manufacturing on its head, they choose trees that were already curved to the lines they needed. Then they assembled that boat, right there on the beach, in between island football and cricket matches, births, funerals, whale hunts and sometimes long naps. When it came time to launch, it was a community affair. They laid down skids and everyone pushed, pulled and partied. That boat and its build was a beautiful throwback to another age.

I was invited on such a boat for the Bequia Easter Regatta, and I could hardly wait. I hoped I wouldn't be too much in the way, that I would do something important and that I wouldn't make any mistakes in front of the home crowd when we tacked the channel. But none of it came to be. That brave little boat lost its wooden mast in stunning fashion, right there while I watched from shore as its intrepid crew sailed through the gusts to come pick me up. With the mast gone, racing was over.

Which led to my ride, instead, on a veritable rocket ship, the 65-foot Swan named *Evrika*, elegantly designed by Sparkman & Stevens and famously owned by Richard Wright, the keyboard player for Pink Floyd.

That yacht had tons of character and infinite stories, but I just wanted to race. I took my job quite seriously when they showed me to my post, a winch larger than any I had ever seen before. I would be trimming the starboard jib sheet.

And here was the owner, the dapper Mr. Wright himself, dressed in white with a straw hat to complete his look of a 1950s gentleman on the Riviera. And there was the rest of our underwhelming crew. Two Frenchmen who matched like twin bookends but were not related, even scrawnier than me yet tasked with the most arduous job on the boat, which was grinding the huge pedestal winches to power things. Both of them kept a cigarette burning in their mouths at all times. And a hairy brute of a man, a pro racer from San Francisco, who looked like he ate babies for breakfast or swung a mace through castle doors. This giant would be trimming opposite me, on the port side jib sheet.

The gun sounded and off we went. As we maneuvered up the race course, we dug well and truly into our roles. The bowman scrambled to hang on, we trimmers flailed and heaved and the French grinders were a blur of Gallic profanity, smoke and rotating arms. Incredible that so much horsepower could come from those tiny bodies.

I'd once heard that there are three places on a racing boat. The bow is Adventureland, the middle is Frontierland and the aft end is Fantasyland. As I hauled on the line for all I was worth, shocked at the speed with which my counterpart outmatched me, I finally understood that saying.

In the back of his boat, Richard Wright reigned cool, calm and collected, steering his craft with one hand exactly like something out of a Nautica or Ralph Lauren advertisement. His straw hat wasn't even ruffled in the gusts.

"Tacking," he would say in upper-class English, smoothly transferring his own cigarette to his other hand while stepping across the boat and switching hands on the wheel, crossing his leg the other direction, a tranquil mirror image of where he'd just been. Meanwhile the rest of us all pulled, spun, ducked and dodged like our lives depended on it.

The owner might decide to tack or jibe on a whim. When he did, the very twitch of his fingertips produced a load or an action which we had to pay dearly for.

Per usual, I was all in, eager to prove myself. I had been taught in lake sailing to call out the puffs as they came to the boat so the helm and trimmer could adjust to them. So I dutifully called out, "Puff, PUFF."

Little did I realize that a boat with such great tonnage did not feel these gusts one bit. But the French lads took up the cry and in their mouths each burst was "Poof, POOF, POOF!" And shreds of this went back to Richard Wright, in whose native country of England that word is an insult. So my eager calls, translated to French and then English street talk, became quite the source of merriment for Richard.

"Tacking," he would sing out.

"Grrraaaaaggghhhh" we would all cry with the effort of our stations.

Me: "Puff!"

The Frenchmen: "POOF"

Richard Wright: "AAHAHAHAHAHAHA"

On one tack, I made a critical mistake. As the line whipped in as fast as I could haul, I missed the extra wrap on the massive winch. It wasn't enough to hold. The sail boomed like a cannon as it filled, and all that force came into my scrappy body. The sheet I was attempting to hold was as big as my wrist. It felt like a wild beast was raging on the other end. To my horror it began to slip and the sail began to flutter.

I was letting the boat down. I was letting Richard down! I would not! I leaned back, hugged the rope against my body, dug my heels into the teak and held on with every fiber of my being. The San Franciscan leered down at me.

"Give me a hand?" I yelped.

He shook his head.

"Looks like a real problem there, mate," he said, and turned his broad back away.

I was about ready to call uncle when a most fortuitous thing occurred. Here came *Hotel California*, a Santa Cruz 70, barrelling at us, a crossing situation. We were the port tack boat. We needed to give way.

"Tacking!" sang Richard Wright with exuberance, dancing the deck once more.

I let go of my line, very happily, with a sneer in the direction of the giant.

Richard was every bit the gentleman he was dressed as, comporting himself with dignity all the race long and taking us for endless Dark & Stormies at the beach bar afterward.

The next day I got an invitation to sail across the Atlantic to the Med with that boat. I turned it down for other good things. In the world of boats, these portals in the flow opened and they closed just as easily. You either made the jump or you didn't, and either way boats and life moved on. You could not dwell on what might have been.

I tried to look up Richard much later, and he was gone, dead of lung cancer. Whenever I hear a Pink Floyd song, I think of the day I was learning the starboard jib sheet on his race boat, and he was blissfully ruling his Fantasyland, tacking up the coastline without a care in the world; those talented hands spinning a wheel instead of playing rock chords, that hat atilt, Richard the quintessential yacht owner, always grinning into the Caribbean breeze.

SEDUCED

THE SEA PRONOUNCES SOMETHING, OVER
AND OVER, IN A HOARSE WHISPER; I CANNOT
QUITE MAKE IT OUT. –ANNIE DILLARD

I found the sea was a temptress with a wild side, always to be pursued but never fully trusted. Yes, she was Mother Ocean, but she was also a black widow. One day she would be intriguing as hell, whispering those sweet nothings in my ear I so wanted to believe; but by the next day she had tricked me again.

Superstition is not a strong enough word to explain what it felt like to stare every day into those unfathomable eyes, knowing her absolute loveliness was matched only by her perfidy.

I came to live by her wishes and whims. I waited on her tides until she was ready for me to pass.

It may have been a one-sided relationship, but that did not mean I was any less taken. I could not get enough. On passages, I watched in adoration as she ran untamed and virile, sporting true blue and achromatic white. Near shore, she was pale and seductive. By night she was aloof and wore a string of moonbeams.

I loved the taste and feel of her. I licked her salt from my lips. Her presence filled the island breeze and I breathed her in greedily. When I was hot, her embrace was ecstasy.

Diving into her from the deck of my sailboat was my longed-for absolution, the best moment of my days. There was always that small hesitation, looking down a little wary, and then my sharp inhale, the abandonment, the push off from my toes and my headfirst penetration, hands-forehead-balls in shattering succession.

Her cool pressure increased as I went deeper, taking that lungful of air down as far as I could go, opening my eyes in her mineral insides, feeling the terror and pleasure of being in this place I didn't belong. That thrill of thalassophobia. Then, reluctantly, looking up to that brightness above and porpoising my body up to break the surface.

When I was sad about nothing, the sea comforted me. When I was angry, she cooled the flames. If I was hungover, a few deep dives would clear my head. If I was mired in myself, swimming through a fantastical school of fish which parted around my body endlessly was the antidote I needed.

On the ocean, I slept every bit as contentedly as I had in my mother's belly. I would fall asleep without effort, feeling the exquisite motion, the gurgle and slap of amniotic fluid, and I would dream of the very best things you can imagine.

The next morning the sea would wake me gently in bits of sensation; that long thundering roll of surf on shore and the seabird's chatter. As the water moved the sailboat beneath me, the sunlight and sea mingled together to make these bright flickering designs on the roof of my cabin, each more beautiful than the last. I could hear the constant crackle of shrimp sounding against the hull, and every so often, borne on a farther current, the otherworldly songs of whales.

In the arms of the ocean, I was immersed in the great mystery itself, attuned to her every pulse, her pains and pleasures, her push and pull.

I'd arrived in those islands with the desperate feeling that I didn't belong anywhere. To that, the sea would always say, "Right here."

She taught me things I am just beginning to understand.

CARNAGE

I f we skippers took a beating, so did the boats. Those long-suffering charter craft went out to do their labors in the great buffeting of the elements, stripped by sun and corrupted by salt water, sometimes dealt a lousy hand by their crew, expected to hold the line against the best destructive efforts of both man and sea.

I had a young family as guests on a catamaran when one engine failed, then the other. It was getting dark and the island lights got further away as I tried to sail that plucky little cat up into the ridiculous wind.

"This is *Sirius*, this is *Sirius*," I kept calling on the radio with no reply, quite a comic ring to hearing it out loud, that is if you weren't being swept out to sea.

There was a local Coast Guard, but one day when my charter boat began filling with water and sinking, I discovered the truth. I called the Coast Guard and finally got someone on the radio.

"Mayday, mayday, mayday, we are sinking and requesting assistance," I said.

"Roger that, captain," the Coast Guard said. "I regret to say that we cannot sail today, because we are not authorized to burn fuel."

The only help was to be found from other charter boats, and all of us skippers, even working for different companies, kept an eye out for each other. Sometimes we towed, and sometimes we were towed. I even rescued a large Coast Guard inflatable which had broken down, the local Coasties helplessly sitting there in matching uniforms and life jackets, my crew and I in ragged shorts, our tiny outboard screaming against the current. I wish someone would have taken a picture of that.

One day I towed a boat in distress and put it on a mooring. Their steering vas kaput, said the two matching German brothers, who were about the size of pro wrestlers. Their boat had twin wheels, one on either side, linked together to the rudder so you could steer from either rail. Now the wheels spun, disconnected.

"Ve need a new boat. This one broken," said Hans.

"Where's the bar?" said Franz. They disappeared.

I asked the wives what had happened.

"Well one of them was pulling on one wheel, and one was on the other..."

I could only imagine the opposing Teutonic forces those two gents could impart. You bet the boat is broke.

Sooner or later, everything would come apart. And as skippers in mid-trip, it was our job to hold it together. We got to know each boat by feel; sweet-talking their quirks through the breakdowns and ill weather, forever with the clock ticking and always in the teeth of that wind.

We whanged on tired windlasses to get the anchor in just one more time. We hotwired water pumps, tricked fridge compressors, patched leaks, dove on tangled props. We coaxed, cussed and muscled those boats. We bled in the bilges.

We were plumbers, electricians and grease monkeys, armed with a few rusted tools, a roll of duct tape and our hands. It was a new class in boat school every day.

Sometimes charter guests ran their own boats, a tenuous arrangement that we called credit card captains.

"Any incidents?" we'd ask the husband on return.

"Nothing," he would always say.

The smart call was to wait and ask the wife after the husband went up the dock. She might have another story.

"Oh, it was a great trip except when we got stuck on that reef and couldn't move all day."

On one job, I was sent south to trade boats with a customer who said his boat didn't work anymore and he wasn't happy about it. The customer is always right and all that, and he allegedly had a boat resume a nautical mile long and had sailed around the world. I had sailed here for only a couple of months, but as soon as I pulled up and tied the replacement boat I'd brought alongside his, I had my doubts. To my inexperienced eye, things looked to be rigged pretty funny. I knocked and knocked on the hull and finally he popped his bleary head up.

"I got your new boat here," I said. "But we're going to need to trade boats in a hurry. I've got to get on the road."

In a place where the sun set promptly at 6 and it was pitch dark by 7, I had a lot of miles to make. I had no idea what was wrong with the crippled yacht, but I had to get it north to the shipyard by sunset. And this world-class yachtsman was moving way too slow.

"Hey, let's do this," I said. "I need you to toss me your bags now."

He was below deck a long time and when he came up, he tried to give me one random handful consisting of women's underwear, a couple of forks and a pack of cheese and crackers. His girlfriend emerged wearing a matching bleary look, not a shred of clothing on and a similarly meager handful of possessions.

"Nope, nope, that's not going to do it," I said.

I could feel the sun rising in the sky already, hot on my neck. I handed over some garbage bags and gave them both 10 minutes to pack.

"So what's the problem with the boat?" I asked.

"Something's wrong with the engine," the yachtsman said. "It just won't go."

Yeah, okay. My spidey sense tingled. So I grabbed a mask and dove on his boat. Mmm-hmm. There was a chunk missing from the aft end of the keel. The rudder was ragged. And the prop shaft was bent sideways like a banana.

I surfaced and grabbed his dingy for a little recon mission. A couple of quick conversations with nearby boats soon confirmed my suspicions.

"Oh, yeah, that boat was on the reef all day. We finally got him off of there at high tide and then we drank a whole bunch of rum to celebrate."

Fair enough. Not the original story, but a classic nonetheless.

Back then to the two boats tied together, where a few lumpy garbage bags of their belongings had now landed on deck.

In the world of wrangling boats, so many things went awry that it's worth relating this thing that worked. The trick here was going to be getting both boats out of the tight anchorage (and away from that reef which now wore a new patch of bottom paint!).

I did the only thing I could conjure up in short order, and that started by rafting the boats together with plenty of fenders, which I'd already done. I helped the hungover yachtsman and lady, now attired, get aboard the new boat along with their garbage bags. I fired up the diesel on the good boat. Then I hopped aboard the crippled boat. I hauled up the anchor chain, vaulted back onto the good boat, and steered us away from boats, rocks and reef. When we were clear of the hazards, I hopped once again (amazing how well I slept after a day like this) onto the reef-damaged boat and pulled the mainsail aloft like a fiend. Now that we had sailpower, I could untie the lines and cut yachtsman loose to go on his merry way and do whatever damage he could do to the new boat. With a backwards wave, I was headed up island as fast as I could possibly go.

Sailing like a madman all day, I pulled into the concrete slip at the boatyard just before dark, and was greeted by one lackadaisical worker with a rum bottle in his pocket. He was the lift operator and it was Christmas Eve. With no propulsion, we were headed for the concrete seawall and nobody on shore to grab a line. So my closing act of that salvage job was diving into the oil-slick workyard waters to push that boat where she belonged. It was yet another scene the cement truck driver would have enjoyed: "Your momma always told you to finish school..."

At times like this a skipper might be tempted to wonder how the math worked out for energy exerted versus Eastern Caribbean dollars earned, but really, it was better not to know.

For as many boats as I helped rescue or rehab, I also left my own marks behind. I was teaching maneuvers in the shallow waters off Carriacou when we hit a coral head at speed. I was hungry as always, eating handfuls of local roasted peanuts out of those green bottles they packed them in. When we thumped that hazard, I staggered and roasted peanuts flew everywhere. I looked up to see more coral heads directly in our path. I'd been paying more attention to my snack than to my navigation. We were flying downwind.

"Let's jibe," I said. It was a move we'd practiced plenty of times and it led to safe water.

The man at the helm stared at me, still rattled from the thump. And as in so many of these cases, it was the woman who stepped up and did the right thing. She grabbed the wheel and spun it over as I tended the mainsheet across. Thanks to her, our jibe was complete, we were back into safe water and we would have no more running aground.

When the boat was in jeopardy, whether by reef, weather or breakdown, people tended to freeze or freak out. A very few guests would actually look straight at me instead and say:

"What do we need to do?"

Usually that person was a woman. In general, I found that women had cooler heads in a crisis, had less ego in the game and took direct action to fix the problem. So, yes, if you ask me, things would in general run better with a woman at the helm; of a company, a country or a boat.

The greatest carnage during my seasons in the Grenadines came at the hands of a gung-ho pack of young Australians who were very unlucky with our boats, not once, but twice. The first boat they took out burned to the waterline on day three. One kid smelled something hot and threw open the engine compartment to look for it, introducing a rush of oxygen and completing the fire triangle with immediate results. Flames went through the boat so fast the kids jumped overboard to escape.

They were a mile or two offshore, but quickly decided they didn't need a signal flare since flames were shooting up and black smoke was roiling. Once lit, the resin in that fiberglass burned hot and fast.

The kids were all rescued by local fishermen, and after traveling elsewhere for a time, decided to come back and get on the horse that threw them.

Their second boat lasted a week before it hit a well-charted rock at night and sank right to the bottom. Once more, all the kids got away without a scrape.

But there would be no third time's a charm for this intrepid crew, since that was the last we ever saw of our young explorers. It was probably just as well. We were already down two good boats and there was no reason to tempt fate any further.

FLOW

THE UNIVERSE IS FULL OF MAGICAL THINGS, PATIENTLY WAIT-
ING FOR OUR WITS TO GROW SHARPER. –EDEN PHILLPOTTS

At the center of each and every trip was a place where time was suspended and the smallest pleasures were sublime. But getting there took days and nautical miles.

In the beginning, the guests would arrive, overdressed, over-eager and over-stimulated. They would tussle over who got the big cabin, keep bumping their heads on the same door frame and smear on way too much or not nearly enough sunscreen that first day.

It would take a while for the frantic pace of back home to wear off. From the shreds of conversations on deck and over dinner those first days, it was clear everyone was still lost in the past. And the past was not always a great place to be.

"You have no idea how hard it was to go on this trip."

"If you hadn't been late, we wouldn't have missed our plane."

"I went sailing once and I was wet, cold and seasick and my dad was yelling at me."

"Our last captain was really funny and a great cook."

"I got so sunburned I just laid in bed and cried."

"I made a ton and then I lost everything."

"I used to be in a lot better shape."

"I got kicked out of Harvard."

"I finally had to leave him."

"My kids must hate me."

"I just kept puking."

"I screwed up."

"I gave up."

But despite any bunkum and balderdash that has come before, no matter how high we've climbed or how far we've fallen, the great gift of any trip is forward motion. And so we sailed on, letting the wind blow the past away.

And in those middle days in the Grenadines we arrived at that marvelous place called now. I knew it was coming and I waited for it with baited breath. In the now, there was less talk, and when we did say anything we said it with a kind of awe. The subject had become much larger than ourselves.

"A turtle swam right up to me."

"That sun feels amazing."

"Look at that moon!"

"I'm jumping in."

"It's so blue."

"Wow."

But I also knew it would not last. Each of these bedazzled days brought us closer to the third act. It got so I would wait, knowing sooner or later someone would break the spell.

"How many days left?"

Bang. Like someone had hit the wrong button on a time-travel machine, we were ripped out of the now and into the uncertain future. That was the tipping point. It was infectious, and I knew that I would not hear anyone talk breathlessly about the wings of a bird in flight again.

But time stops for no sailor, and the show must go on.

"We fly out Friday."

"Wait, that's just three more days."

"I can't forget my phone charger this time."

"Babe, you really need to find those passports."

"What time do you guys have to be at the airport?"

"I hope it's not snowing when we have to drive home."

"Did you remember to tell the dogsitter what we're doing?"

"I'm really not looking forward to this court case on Monday."

"I can't wait for our next vacation a year from now."

It was time. I watched as they ramped up their pace and their volume again, packed up their bags, dressed up to beat the cold and to match their rightful roles, and went away, sometimes shedding a tear, and always casting that one lingering glance back at the sea.

TIPPED

MAN IS THE ONLY ANIMAL FOR WHOM HIS EXISTENCE IS
A PROBLEM WHICH HE HAS TO SOLVE. –ERICH FROMM

"**I** don't see why there is this tipping."

My charter guest looked down at me through swollen eyes over a broad sunburned nose and chin. It was day eight of a ten-day trip, and once again, I was hearing about the tipping.

He was a bullheaded captain of industry from one of the northern European countries. I was simply the temporary captain of his boat, one who happened to survive on the tips he so despised.

Early in the tour I'd noticed a conspicuous absence of anything resembling a tip in our encounters with cab drivers, dockhands and restaurant staff. Now he was complaining again, in what seemed to be a preemptive move to head off any cash changing hands between us at his departure.

"It makes no sense, the tipping," he said. "When I eat, I pick what I want, I get the food, I pay. When I want a boat, I find a good price, I get a boat. That's it."

He shrugged his meaty shoulders.

"I pay for a captain, I get a captain," he said. "You tell me, why the tipping?"

When I'd started running boats, I'd been overjoyed with a hundred dollars here and there. Now after the graces of generous clients who'd sometimes gifted thousands at trip's end to show their appreciation, my expectations ran higher.

My job was always to care for the passengers and the boat, no matter what. I didn't work for gratuities, but I sure began counting on them. I came to judge the trip by the tip. If someone didn't leave one, or gave a paltry amount, I was annoyed with them and doubtful of myself.

Just what was it, I would wonder, that I had failed to execute during 16-hour days of babysitting grown people while performing a series of magic tricks? After lobster on the beach, dinghy rides for the kids, fishing off the stern, barracuda on the grill, sailing lessons, secret anchorages and sugary beaches, all delivered in safety, comfort and fun, what possible rabbit remained that I had not pulled out of my hat?

There did appear to be a regional aspect to tipping, much like the attitudes in general about itinerary, weather, malfunctions and first-world inconveniences.

West Coast clients seemed in general most enthused, less anxious and more generous. These qualities diminished as you moved east; not always, but as a rough rule of thumb.

Even the California surgeon whose Nikon I dropped into the ocean handed me a stack of bills as I bid his family farewell.

Wives/daughters/girlfriends would give me a heartfelt hug, maybe a kiss or two or sometimes pinch me on the bum as their father/husband/boyfriend shook my hand and handed me a roll of hundred dollar bills.

"I want your job, no, I want your life," those doctors, lawyers, investment bankers and CEOs told me, time and again.

So here I was, staring at the enemy of all tipping, and what did I have to say?

The image that came to mind was of me setting up his wife's water toy every morning. She was fearful of the ocean and didn't like to swim, but did enjoy bobbing behind the boat in this contraption. It fell my way to inflate the thing, and since I didn't have a pump, I used my lungs until I was faint-headed, thinking to myself, here it is again, the glamorous life of a yacht captain.

I wish I could have waxed eloquent, standing up and delivering a movie-worthy speech in which I defended the honor of all front line service folks who labor away with a smile in the face of impossibility. Instead I just mumbled something forgettable, and he just grunted. I'd already figured there would be no gold at this end of this charter's rainbow and that was fine.

When we arrived back at base, I finessed the boat against the blistering crosswinds and into a tight space. That move alone, protecting my client's safety and his boat damage deposit, was worth a lot. But he was right, that was my job. I tied the boat up right, a final ritual, the formal end to another trip.

When I went below to grab my seabag, I noticed something strange. My guest was packing every single bit of leftover food, intending to carry it away with him. He piled up condiments, cans, fresh odds and bits, the things that normally would be given away to the dock staff and their families to take home. I'd never seen anyone do that before.

"Here, you want these?"

Now he was waving some leftover items at another boat across the dock.

Well, there's some faint generosity, after all, I mused, before I heard him negotiating and realized that this business mogul was trying to drive up the going rate on a couple half-used rolls of paper towels and a six-pack of TP. He was impossible.

Yet, like so many of my island encounters, this one had an unexpected ending. As mom, daughter and dad stood outside the taxi van and I said my goodbyes, I saw a hesitation in my client's brash step and a tremor in his mighty hand. It went in and out of his pocket a couple times before emerging painfully once more, as if his shoulder had just been dislocated.

Five hundred American dollars went from his hand to mine. He grimaced, shook his head and boarded the taxi.

His daughter gave me a kiss and a hug, got on her tiptoes and whispered in my ear.

"I've never seen Daddy tip anyone, ever," she said.

Dollar for dollar, his would forever have to be considered the biggest gratuity of them all.

BURNED

It's hard to put a finger on the moment I knew I'd finally hit the wall.

Was it the clients? Watching the same guy hold the same freezer door open again as all that precious cold air rushed out while he kept digging slowly around like a bear looking under a log? (Finally I learned to appoint a fridge captain, picking the most OCD person on the boat to organize the fridge and freezer and then to chase everyone else out).

Was it Chip Lady eating every last one of the Doritos so lovingly and then licking all her fingers one by one? Was it all the chatter, that talk-talk-talking about nothing whatsoever? Was it sitting and waiting in the tender under the blazing sun while yet another guest went back onto the boat yet again looking for sunscreen/phone/bug spray/who-knows-what?

Sometimes I just couldn't get the guests going in the same direction, making me wonder darkly how a species that had survived, thrived and achieved so much could not execute the most basic of tasks.

Was it gear failure? I'd pull the outboard engine starter rope until I thought my arm would come out of its socket. Fix the same water pump I'd fixed the week before. Unclog the head! Or I'd grab anything else important and it would fail right there in my hands.

Was it weather? I'd set something down and the wind would blow it away. Try to light the barbecue and the wind would snuff it out. Schedule a day at the beach and the rain would soak us all. We'd spend that week anchored in the swells, halyards clanging all uneasy night long. Was it answering questions again about what I guessed the weather would do today? (I finally appointed a weather captain for that, too).

At times, low on sleep, weary of body and brain, it all seemed a conspiracy to foil the captain's very simplest hopes and plans. I. Just. Want. It to WORK!

One of my pressure valves was movement. With the anchor secured, swim ladder down ("The pool's open!" was my standard line), and boat chores done for the afternoon, I'd jump head-first into the welcome cool and silence of the ocean. I would swim to the beach, where I had a series of sprints, punches and pushups to take the edge off.

My other trick was dropping the guests ashore (once everyone was finally dressed, dosed with mosquito repellent, in possession of their wallets and phones and... come-on-already!)

I'd beg out of their invariable offer to join them for dinner.

"I've got to go back and keep an eye on things," I'd say.

Then I'd gun the throttle back to the empty boat. There, I would wear no shirt, answer no questions and listen to nothing except my own music. I'd gaze out over my watery realm and just plain be. I might savor a peanut butter sandwich.

After three hours of this introverted bliss, I would yank the outboard to life again and pick up my guests at the dock. In their late-night condition, it was a pure slapstick to get everybody loaded into the tippety tender.

Then I would drive back unfailingly through the dark. It was one of my favorite parts of the day. Standing at the stern, night vision keen, I could always navigate back to the one correct boat in the anchorage amid all the others. People were always amazed at that skill and I was, too.

The other satisfaction was in timing the landing; cutting the power back at just the right time and turning the tender so we slid perfectly into place. It felt good every time.

"He's done that before," someone would always say.

Depending on my mood, the day's events and whether or not I got on with the guests, I would stay up for a few stories. Or I'd just excuse myself to my hot and sticky cabin (the crew gets the smallest one with no airflow), read a book (they started out highbrow and became more mindless as the season progressed), scribble in my journal (heartfelt nonsense) or if nothing else, listen to my beloved music.

I had these whole fantasy scenarios if I couldn't sleep. I could replay movies in my head, scene by scene. My favorite go-to escape, however, was an elaborate one in which I beamed off the boat and picked up my girl in a fast car.

I'd sent her to the spa where she was all pampered and polished. She'd have that gorgeous body dressed to the nines and I had on an Italian suit, and we went out into the evening to a restaurant in the middle of a foreign city, to a table for two far from any sun, sea, sand or passengers.

I could picture exactly what we ordered and how it tasted. I knew how she touched her neck, how she smiled at me in that way.

Then we drove the streets to our hotel, going fast, enjoying the G forces on every corner in that car, tossing the keys to the valet and taking the elevator to the top floor suite. It was a fine, high place where no sailors could ever find me. All the lights of the city twinkled below. The room was vast and elegant. The air was cool, the sheets were cool and her skin was just right...

Then a noise would sound close by my ear: A water pump running dry. BRRRRRRRRRRRRRR. Or a loud kerBANG. "Where's the cookies?"

Don't make the captain come out there! Burnout found me jumpy, irritable, crazed and sleep-deprived, ready to strangle the next offender or just get on a plane myself and never, ever see another boat.

SMITTEN

THEY SLIPPED BRISKLY INTO AN INTIMACY FROM WHICH
THEY NEVER RECOVERED. –F. SCOTT FITZGERALD

L ife has a way of sending the antidote when you need it most, and the Brannigan trip was just what the doctor ordered.

"I think you'll like this one," said the manager, winking at me. He knew I was so fried I'd been begging for a break. I suspect he'd shuffled the rotation to get me these particular clients.

"It's a private charter, just two people, and he's ordered some really good wine," he said, a connoisseur himself. "The bloody wine's worth more than you and the boat."

Whatever. I was done. I'd had it with guests, boats, beaches and bars. And yet...

Down the dock walked a dark-haired beauty, heading my way.

Behind her came a sharp-dressed man, presumably the husband, followed by the dock crew carrying the woman's considerable bags and many aforementioned cases of fine wines.

We hit it off immediately.

They were a sophisticated pair of expats who lived in the islands full time. They were younger than me, groomed and attired in the manner of wealth. I found him wickedly funny, a man of the world, and I found her increasingly captivating.

Ben and Athena. What great chemistry and what a trip we shared. Together, the three of us had about as good a time as you ever could. We sailed the boat with pleasure and sought out the best places on each island. We laughed 'till it hurt.

We sailed at night, strictly banned but a splendid rush. We anchored where no boats normally went, just us three and the sound of waves on the reef beyond. We consumed more G&Ts than was necessary.

It was the one trip I didn't want to see end. At the finish, we stayed up all night talking and carrying on, toasting the sunrise with the last of the good bubbly, making the ride last as long as we could.

"Here's the deal," Ben said. "We're going to buy a boat and you're going to run it."

It was a pipe dream and we all knew it. I gave him my number anyway and shook his hand goodbye. When Athena hugged me, I didn't want to let go. Her faint sweat and perfume was intoxicating, an aftershock of it lingering on my skin. They were off to board a private jet, and here I was back in my sweltering cabin with the broken fan and the leaky hatch.

But I wasn't the same.

Those two saved my tired sailor's soul. With the Brannigan trip, I found myself cured of burnout and back in the game. I was under the boyhood spells again, newly intrigued with the possibilities and places boats could go.

BIGGER

I WAS ON THE VERGE OF JUMPING INTO ONE OF THOSE
HOLES IN LIFE OUT OF WHICH WE EMERGE A BIT TATTERED
AND BLOODY, THOUGH WE REMAIN SURE NONETHELESS
THAT WE HAD TO MAKE THE JUMP. —JIM HARRISON

A s the seasons passed in the islands, and I kept on running my share of humble charters and deliveries, one question continued to burn: What was life like on those sleek yachts moored next door or sliding past on the horizon?

One especially stunning boat caught my eye as I came into the Tobago Cays. It was a massive sailboat with classic looks, modern build and design; undeniably sexy. I drove by it in my small tender, marveling at the mirror-perfect reflection in the hull and the work it must take to keep it that way.

"Hey," I heard from way above.

At the high rail was a blonde lady, waving heartily.

"Come on up!"

Like a sailor's best dream, here was the finest boat in the anchorage with a fine woman beckoning me aboard. I could only go.

She greeted me at the steps, and I recognized the lady who'd befriended us while she stayed at a small resort on our island.

"Come on up and see the boat," she said.

I was wearing just an old pair of surf shorts and no shirt and everyone I could see was dressed impeccably. But I didn't want to miss the chance, so I tied up the dinghy and came aboard, feeling self-conscious without my clothes.

She introduced me to the owner. I'd heard the story already; how he'd worked steadily in his father's business while his older brother got the girl and a sailboat and went off to sea. She was that girl, and it turns out this younger brother had always been secretly in love with her. Remarkably, after all these years, after the business had finally sold and he'd made his millions, he'd built this boat and come looking for her. We humans are a strange and obsessive lot indeed.

The owner was an affable guy who toured me around the boat himself instead of handing me off to his crew. His pride and enjoyment was evident. His yacht was splendid in every way.

But what I really wanted was a peek behind the scenes. I kept asking for the captain and was finally directed to where he was barricaded in his cabin and didn't want to come out. I persisted, and he finally let me in.

"You've gotta tell me. What's it like running a boat this fine?" I said.

I coaxed it out of him in bits.

He'd been onsite in Europe all three years of the vessel's build; he'd launched her, delivered her and knew her every secret. That boat had taken over his life. There was no time off. Running a crew of 18 was a full job in itself, especially when the crew was young and footloose.

"If the boss calls and says we have 10 people for dinner, and my kitchen staff falls in love with someone ashore and doesn't show up, I've got a real problem," the captain said.

I noticed his nervous tics.

"Now the owner is starting to talk about doing charters to help pay some expenses, and I don't want to get back into the charter business again. I've served my time."

"But still," I said, "You have to admit it must be the best feeling in the world, driving this boat into a new harbor."

"It's pretty great," he managed a smile. "But it's all at a price."

He grew nostalgic: "The best boat job I ever had was running a simpler boat with my girlfriend and maybe one deckhand. What are you sailing?"

I confessed my lowly command, the old 45-foot cat I was delivering. There, running the ragged edge of the game in surf shorts, I felt underdressed, unprofessional and underwhelming. The captain cracked a smile.

"So you're just going to dinghy back, turn up the rock & roll and make yourself some mac and cheese for dinner?" he said. "That sounds so good right now..."

His shoulders slumped, just a fraction.

"Nah, it's great, no complaints," he said. "I get paid so much I really can't leave anymore. I've got two houses and some women to support and the kids in private schools."

We sat there and contemplated each other's existence for a moment, the wild-haired, half-naked me and the well-groomed, tidy him.

Then his intercom went off and made him jump.

"Captain?" It was a woman's voice. "Would you get up here? I can't get this thing working."

"I'll be right there."

He shrugged and saw me out.

On my way off the yacht I saw the woman who'd beckoned me aboard. She was suntanning on the aft deck, enjoying the ride most definitely but in her own cabin, she made a point of saying, and with the intention of going her own way come the end of the trip. Her hair in the wind spelled a freedom of its own. All that boat, and still there was no spark.

I thanked the owner for his time and complimented his boat.

He returned the compliment straightaway.

"I'd trade it right now to be in the kind of shape you're in," he said to my surprise. "So where you headed now?"

"Well, I'm going back to that tiny boat over there, make some mac and cheese for dinner and crank up the music," I said.

"That sounds absolutely incredible," said the owner of the $50 million yacht with a wistful grin, and shook my hand good-bye.

MADNESS

WE ARE CHASIN' THE MOON, JUST RUNNING WILD
AND FREE; WE ARE FOLLOWING THROUGH, EVERY
DREAM AND EVERY NEED. –THE CORRS

T urns out Ben Brannigan was serious about buying a boat.

"I've found her," came his cultured voice over the phone, excitement in every word. "Just need you to go pick her up."

Overnight, the game had gotten bigger and more intense.

I flew to Newport, Rhode Island, and had his dream sloop surveyed and sea trialed. He'd picked a luxurious beauty and she passed with flying colors.

The boat and I spent the obligatory time in a boatyard as I pitted my punchlist of jobs against the clock and the season. Winter was coming soon to New England, and as a reminder, I had a daily call from Don Street, the iconoclastic salty dog of Caribbean infamy, who was also our insurance agent.

"What the devil are you doing in the yard putting in these Vacuflush heads and all this other nonsense?" Don would rant.

"You don't need it! You get a big hand-powered bilge pump

loaded, and you carry those boards for when the windows break out and you get that bloody boat moving south!"

My crew arrived but, like sailors immemorial, refused to leave without a proper ceremony to rechristen the yacht. Athena hoisted a bottle of champagne and we did the right toasts to the ship, to those who'd sailed her before, to her new crew and to her new name, *Marigold.*

I got a green light from Commander's Weather, giving us a time and an hour to leave the dock. They timed the kinetic moods of the Gulf Stream perfectly so that we motored across in flat conditions. Twelve hours later, the Stream was a mess and on the radio we heard that our sister ship was knocked down and swamped, ripping a bunch of gear off the deck.

The wind filled again and rocketed us on down the way. We were somewhere in the Bermuda Triangle one night when the boat swung straight around and began driving itself back to Newport again. When I checked the chart plotter, the system had inexplicably reversed. No amount of reboots or tech support on the sat phone could unravel the mischief that the Triangle had done. In the end we tricked the autohelm to go to Tortola by telling it to drive backwards the rest of the way.

It was a rollicking passage of less than nine days. We checked into another boatyard for yet another project. I'd promised Athena that she could have her boat by Christmas and there wasn't much time to spare.

In Tortola, I made the mistake of picking up an outboard too big for me and hustled it down the dock. The next day, as I bent upside down and inspected the bilges as part of my pre-departure check, a paralyzing shock went off between my shoulder blades and dropped me to the cabin floor. Turned out I'd separated a rib. But we had our weather window and it was go time. Plus I'd promised Athena.

Going upwind for days was no fun, especially with my back screaming every time we dropped off another square wave. I wedged myself in my bunk, furious, while the owner and his friend stood watches. When I heard yelling I tumbled on deck to see that our tender had separated from its davits and was flailing around behind the boat in the pitch black night.

It was the captain's problem now.

Like a crazed monkey, I took the line in my teeth, leaped onto the out-of-control tender and lashed things back where they belonged. There was no pain. It was one of those fine moments that cuts through everything with the clarity of what must be done. Mindless response and into the fray; a purity I hope everyone gets to experience sometime in life.

On the day before Christmas Eve, we sailed into the harbor, lovely Athena waving like her Greek namesake, the patroness of heroes.

The owner and friend hastily departed, with a "good luck!" and a clap on the back, and now I saw why. Once more it was time to earn my dues. Here came the object of my fears, the customs officials, and my knees were knocking all over again.

Two uniformed men came aboard, and I winced as they kept their shoes on and trampled the clean teak.

"Do you have anything to declare?"

In fact I sure did, but I wasn't going to say so. Before we'd left America with the boat, Athena had flown up for an impressive shopping spree. The aft cabin was packed to the gills with so many luxury household goods that the stern of the boat was noticeably lower. On this island, every item was subject to a hefty import tax, so I was now in charge of a boatload of contraband.

I felt like the man in Poe's *The Tell-Tale Heart,* just waiting for that cabin door to burst open, cascading televisions, appliances and Jimmy Choo stilettos and sealing my fate.

"I need to declare two bottles of Johnny Walker Black Label," I managed to say instead, gesturing to the cabin table.

A captain friend had once casually mentioned that if I ever cleared into this island I should bring exactly that. At the time I'd thought it was a curiously specific instruction. Now I was putting his advice to the test.

Neither of the officers even glanced toward the bottles. Instead, the lead man asked me to open the refrigerator, of all places, where he made a thorough inspection of the string cheese. Out of the corner of my eye, I saw a quick movement, nothing more.

With the fridge approved, we turned around. The whiskey was gone as if by magic trick. Only the junior officer holding a briefcase remained. The senior officer smiled.

"Welcome to the island, sir," he said. "Have a nice day."

So *Marigold* arrived at her new homeport, and the madness ensued in earnest: Champagne cruises up and down the coast, late nights that bled into the next days, sometimes ending with us kicked out of posh resorts by an embarrassed staff.

Ben was increasingly mercurial and brooding. Athena drove us through narrow streets at speed, her fingers tapping on the steering wheel and her eyes flashing at me in the rearview.

The physical longing in her music was a fitting soundtrack for our headlong rush into the void together; for a whirlwind existence in which rock stars, race car drivers and models came and went.

The moneyed class here escaped taxes, flew private 747s, bought expensive ponies and otherwise curated their own charmed and bleak fantasy.

What we really needed was to get out of town. So we left all that commotion behind for the optimism of sailing somewhere real instead. Ben seemed to come out from under his cloud, and Athena promised we would definitely have fun.

It was nearly as good as those first times we'd all three had together, as we cruised back up through the islands: anchoring under the Pitons of St. Lucia, closing down the clubs of Guadeloupe and racing other yachts around Antigua.

At the end of my contract, we tied up at Nelson's Dockyard below the old fort, where many captains before me had come and gone.

And where did I measure up? Indeed, I had risen to the task and run the dream yacht. But who was I now, and what had become of the lad who'd eagerly taken this job only months ago?

This season had been more risky than any storm, more compelling than any new landfall. Somehow the Brannigans had managed to rachet up everything I loved about this boat life to an unbearable degree.

My great weakness, I now understood, was my addiction to sensation and experience. Each in their own way, Ben and Athena had managed to know and satisfy that craving. They had flooded my veins with massive doses of my drug of choice, and I had begged for more.

Now I had the hopeless junkie shakes. I had to get clean.

It was time for me to get on a plane while any shred of sanity remained. So I went from the yachting scene to the wilds.

This is how my last Caribbean season ended. With Ben Brannigan's boat cash in my pockets, I fled to the Sian Ka'an Biosphere Reserve, a far-flung watery wilderness between Mexico and Belize. There, I stayed with my long-awaited lovely wife in a little house on stilts, and I hired Antonio to take me bonefishing. Every day, my guide and I cruised the flats looking for phantoms.

My soul, bankrupt and split open, was slowly soothed by the long, fast panga rides at dawn into nothingness, the wide skies and empty flats, those profound conversations with Antonio in simple Spanish.

Cormorants burst from the waves as if water itself was taking flight. Storms lashed the sea. We peered into a blue hole where all manner of creatures circled way down there as if in dreams. Those bonefish, when I finally managed to land them, were primeval wonders in my grateful, exhausted hands.

Way out there, I felt a bit of something like happiness returning.

WALTER

ANY KINDNESS I CAN SHOW TO ANY FELLOW CREATURE,
LET ME DO IT NOW. LET ME NOT DEFER OR NEGLECT IT FOR
I SHALL NOT PASS THIS WAY AGAIN. –WILLIAM PENN

There's a picture that means more these days to me than ever. We are two men from vastly different places, connected by a boat. Walter has his head tipped back in laughter. I grin from ear to ear, very tan. It was my first winter in the islands, an innocent and amazing time.

I think about Walter sometimes and wonder why he made such an impression. When you've spent a good part of your life as untethered as I have, those passing connections count for much and last for life. Part of it was the setting; his "office" was one of the finest on the planet. But there was much else.

Walter was the de facto lead boat boy of one of the most classic and spectacular sailing destinations in the world. He and his mates, at the helm of colorful wood runabouts with ancient outboards, played a critical role in a remote anchorage.

He and his mates would guide you in past the unmarked reefs, make sure your hook was set and bring supplies. They sold T-shirts, lobster, bread, ice and sodas. Anything you needed, Walter could probably fire up his beat-up engine, disappear over the curve of the water and return in an hour or two with exactly that. The other boat guys all respected Walter, so once you connected with him, they all watched out for you.

Talk to someone who'd sailed here, and chances are they'd remember a good chat with Walter, his voice deep and gravelly, his smile huge and flashing a gold front tooth. It became a part of the experience of arrival in a place so real.

Walter was born in those islands, and he didn't have a lot of economic opportunity, but he was motivated to advance in life, so he went to sea as a fairly young man as a deckhand, worked hard, saved his money and then came home, bought property, built a house and had a family.

Once I was up the mast hammering away on a seized furling drum when a squall came and began flogging the unfurled sail. The boat strained at its anchor and I was getting good and thrashed up there. The charter guests looked on with wide eyes. They didn't know what to do.

Walter did. He came shooting across the anchorage in his skiff and vaulted with great athleticism onto the deck.

"What you need, Skip?" he said in that big, reassuring voice.

He jumped into the fray, wrapped his arms around that flogging sail like a prizefighter going into battle and saved the day.

Sometime later I went to his house as a guest for dinner and met his wife and family. His happiness and energy were absolutely contagious. He was the living epitome of the T-shirts he sold: "Sail Fast, Live Slow."

Walter knew he was always welcome to tie up his skiff and hop on board, where I would offer him juice, water or soda (he didn't drink alcohol) and introduce him around with pride to my guests. These reciprocal acts of human kindness cut across all else; they meant and continue to mean a great deal to me.

The other day came word that Walter, shot through with cancer, had finally greeted his very last boat and was gone. This news hit harder than I expected.

He was my first welcome, my hero to the rescue, an excellent host, proud dad and businessman and the master of his watery domain. I will miss his gold-toothed smile, his booming voice and his positive energy.

Walter and his ways stood for something special, a purity of life and a freedom that sailors have always sought and that we continue to seek.

In Walter, I see the reasons why I came to the islands, and the ways they stole my heart.

Farewell, my legendary friend.

ISLANDS

A NOMAD I WILL REMAIN FOR LIFE, IN LOVE WITH DISTANT
AND UNCHARTED PLACES. –ISABELLE EBERHARDT

These days, I sail very different seas than the Caribbean. My home waters are a fresh blue lake in the mountains of Idaho in the summer and the sunny Pacific Mexico coastline in winter. But the Grenadines are forever tattooed on my sailor's soul.

I can close my eyes and see every waypoint, hazard and harbor. I can tell you things only seafarers know.

I first saw those islands as obstacles, with their reefs and currents I had to figure out how to avoid. But as time passed they became my allies. I came to trust the holding in this anchorage and the shelter over there. I learned their ways and their confidences.

Blindfold me today, and I can still guide you into their trickiest places. I know where the wind gusts, where the anchor drags and where the seas run rough. I also know where to swim with sea turtles and where to spend the night under the stars without another soul around. I know a reef where we can freedive way, way down to where that big old grouper lives, where we can swim face to face with octopus, triggerfish and barracuda.

Each one of those exquisite islands has its own character, and its own characters.

St. Vincent is the mother island, the northernmost and biggest of the chain, where I first landed and lived. There I once tried to climb to the top of a volcano with two Rastafarian guides who were clearly lost from the beginning. By the time we stumbled into yet another ganja farm, the plants towering high above our heads, the sun plummeting and the summit trail nowhere in sight, these cousins finally conceded defeat. They badly wanted to be tour guides and I was their first client, and possibly their last. They had no car so we rode the public dollar vans back down the island. It was the best day ever.

The charter base where I worked was a microcosmic study in class with its white owners, brown managers and black laborers. Most of those employees had grown up in a hut with dirt floors, a tin roof and no running water. They were some of the best human beings I've ever encountered. Their measures of time and wealth were so different from mine. After payday, they wouldn't show up for work for a few days. They would also never fail to help a stranger when they could.

The charter base, and the island itself, would often be without power, or water or internet, and sometimes all three things in a trifecta of haplessness. I was fortunate to be part of so many island dramas here, both grand and slapstick.

I was there when the Germans came in. Their flotilla streamed the flags of their various football teams and family crests. Their boats filled every mooring and every dock, and the Germans stormed cheerfully ashore, very thirsty.

"Jack Daniels!" said the lead German.

We'd just had payday and most of the staff had vanished. So it was big, beaming Sandra the cook and I dispensing the whiskey as fast as we could and rustling up food.

"Light de fire!" Sandra would order, and I'd hustle to do so. "Bring de pan!"

That night was the one and only time I've ever worked in food service. At Sandra's lead, with both of us sweating, bumping and grinding in that tiny kitchen, I cooked, carried and poured like a man possessed.

"Born on the Bayou!" sang the German.

He carried a guitar and had Fogerty's raw vocals down so well it was uncanny to watch.

Much later that night, I watched a woman in a black dress step with authority from the dock to her boat and completely miss it. She went straight down into the bay and the night guard and I fished her out, whereupon she cocked her wet head elegantly, lipstick and dignity intact and her cocktail glass still held aloft.

"I believe I'm due for a drink," she said.

I can still taste the sweet water from a coconut hacked open by cutlass; the mango so ripe it fell off the tree into my hands, juice flowing down my chin and the surprising spiciness of it. I can taste the curry, the snapper, the callaloo, the rotis, the bois bande ("mek you strong and mek babies all night long"), the goat water, the shocking homebrewed rum.

I recall fabled Mustique, a private island where the one percenters cavorted without fear of the paparazzi. At a time when the tabloids were delighted to have "caught" Russell Crowe with Meg Ryan, I saw him on Mustique, and he winked at me as he drove past in his mini-moke. The woman wrapped tightly around him was exactly the opposite of Meg.

This was an island of high life and hijinks. A fellow captain's kids played soccer with Mick Jagger as their goaltender. I would see Mick sitting in his corner at Basil's Bar in his floppy hat, sipping a daiquiri, female attention never far from hand.

Basil's Bar was the scene of the wildest party I've ever been swept up into, with Basil himself holding court, handsomely attired in a white robe and caftan, a woman on each arm. It was his birthday party and reason enough for excess of every kind, a night of anything goes. At some point there were fireworks out over the lagoon, reflected in the stoned eyes of supermodels.

Mustique, no matter how high the price of the mooring balls or increasingly discouraging the harbormaster, was always a fun visit with guests. People had never seen anything like it and neither had I.

We would ride past those island estates to swim on a dazzling beach as white and fine as powdered sugar, then later walk up the hill to Firefly, where we joined the glitterati with expensive rum punches on the balcony as a man in a tux played the piano and we watched the sun slide into the sea. It was the very same view for saints and sinners, rich and broke, the demented and the sane, although this far south in the Caribbean, those lines were always blurred.

The Tobago Cays were utterly mind blowing. The first time I stopped there, I remember watching one shooting star after another explode and leave trails down the sky. With no landmass to break the wind, it felt like the boat was flying through those stars even though we were anchored. It was the Leonids meteor shower, and I stayed awake until dawn it was so good. The next day I thought I'd discovered a new species of seabird, white on top and turquoise blue underneath. As I came down from my arrival high I realized it was just the intense color of the water all around us, reflected upwards.

On Union Island, I scrambled to the thumb-shaped high point and found a big iguana on the summit. He shook his head up and down at me, and I did the same at him. I sat there for a long time in this bearded lizard's company, looking out at his lofty dominion. I was nearing the end of my time in these islands, and this was now my domain, too.

From here I could see the kiteboard sails buzzing around Happy Island, a little bar jutting out of the bay and built up entirely of conch shells. I could see the reefs I'd squeezed between, the decrepit boat where the naked old liveaboard would come out on deck and hurl her French curses at you if you anchored anywhere near, the airport where I'd once flown a combative client out to get her off the boat, and that customs office where I'd made many more contributions to the local charity as I passed through over the seasons.

I looked out to Petit Martinique, the place we called smuggler's island. Boats would wash up there in the middle of the night, their cargo mysteriously gone by morning. When law and order tried to intervene in this lucrative trade, the pirates burned the station down and spray painted **Coast Guard Go Home** on the blackened walls. On smuggler's island you could always reprovision the boat with top shelf liquor of every kind at a fraction of the ordinary cost. You could also buy the local moonshine out of a Thermos with a spigot.

Next to it was Petit St. Vincent, where villas went for thousands a night with the utmost in privacy. If you wanted room service, you raised a little flag on your roof. One memorable evening, my charter guests and I had been told to hurry up and drink our rum punches. We were quickly chased out of that beach bar, but not for bad behavior this time. They were clearing every table in the place, and we soon found out why.

Back on our boat, we watched an enormous silver yacht slide into the anchorage. Out of its stern slipped two grey inflatable tenders, which began to cruise in formation through the anchored boats. One inflatable pulled up right behind us, and two men who looked like brothers with their broad shoulders, close-cropped hair and intense faces called out in a friendly but professional manner. They looked our boat over pretty good, then moved on.

Now we were curious, and put binoculars on the yacht, but never saw a thing. Right after it was too dark to make out details, a long, low craft jetted away from the yacht, flanked by the two inflatables. They flew straight to the bar we'd vacated.

"Wow," said one of my guests. "That's someone who doesn't want to be seen."

"Nope," said another guest. "That's someone who doesn't want to get shot."

We never did figure out who it was. There was no name on the yacht and it did not show up on marine traffic. Out here, we shared the waters with all kinds of craft and all manner of pursuits; the rock stars and the washed up, the vagrants and the kingpins, the wannabes and the real things. If you wanted to escape someone or impress someone you came to the islands. That could have been a princess, a president or a gangster. It might have been anyone.

From way up here with my lizard friend, I could see Palm

Island, where renowned yachtsman Johnny Coconut had settled and planted his namesake trees, then built three houses in a row; one for him, one for his wife and another for his mistress. Palm Island had been my place to escape and run the trail around the island, until one day I was accosted by a security guard ringing his bicycle bell.

"Private property," he said, articulating the words.

"I know, but I always run this trail."

The guard man shook his head and his gold front teeth gleamed in a sad smile.

"New management," he enunciated, and ushered me gently out.

I understood, It was the same story that was happening everywhere. Johnny Coconut had died and a corporation had taken over. The future would be more managed and less colorful than the past.

The tiniest island in the Grenadines is Mopion, a postage stamp of sand that appears and disappears in the hurricanes. It was the ultimate coup to get my guests ashore there alone before the other charter skippers arrived, or worse yet, the big charter cats. It was my mission to get that perfect photo of my guests on their own private island, without the riffraff. And of course to those other captains, we were the riffraff.

Mopion has one little palm-thatched stand with a bottle opener on it. The only other things on Mopion are those things you bring with you. I've seen it as happy as can be as newlyweds kicked up surf. I've seen it violent in a fistfight and boisterous with a tackle football game, the end zones the ocean on each side. I've seen people screaming at each other, miserable in paradise. Mopion is the ultimate reminder that every place is exactly what we make it.

But no island will ever be closer to my heart than Bequia. I hesitate even to try to write about the place, because I fear I won't have the words.

I think of dancing close together, barefoot in the sand on New Year's Eve while boats in the harbor fired their flares up into the night, of walking home hand in hand up narrow roads in the dense warm dark.

Bequia is where I married my true love on a beach, stumbling and giggling over our lines. It's where our friends drove us around the island in the back of a taxi truck decorated with frangipani flowers, honking the horn while people came out of their homes and waved. We borrowed a boat and ran away down island for a honeymoon that has never really ended.

When I returned from the sea Rebecca would swim out to my boat like a beautiful mermaid, surprising the guests. I would always find an excuse to stop for the night at Bequia. I would find her at our little house and wrap her in my arms, and she would make me dinner, our simple fare by candlelight so much tastier than the finest of restaurants.

It was the one night of the trip where I bent the rules, deserted my captain's post and slept ashore. And who can blame me? But after weeks on the ocean, it was always strange to be in a real bed again. My body was mystified by the absence of movement. Every rainsquall on the roof would bring me out of bed to check on the anchor. In the mornings, there would be Rebecca's fine tanned body sleeping next to me beneath the mosquito net, island dogs barking down the valley, sunrise through our window, salt breeze coming up from the bay.

Bequia was fireflies and tortoises. It was skinny dips and

rum drinks at Friendship Bay, body surfing the rough black sand beach on the windward side, lazy lovely days at Lower Bay and otherwordly drift dives at Moonhole. It was floating in the ocean, watching extraordinary clouds overhead, hearing that sound in our ears underwater that the surf makes as it moves pebbles across the bottom, feeling the salt drying on our skin in the sunshine.

Most of all, it was our friends in all their colors, voices and ways. It was island speak. The descriptions were lively and the cadence musical and there was always a gentle avoidance of specific time and distance.

How far was that beach? "Not so far."

How long before the thing arrived? "Not so long."

When would someone return? "She go to come back."

Or the ultimate reply to anything else: "Me nah know."

Taking something without asking was "teefing." If a thing was broken it was "mash up."

The lady who watched me hop around, trying to dance, and finally grabbed me to show the proper way, saying, "You doan move your feets bwoy, you gots to move ya HIPS."

Pashel my windsurfing buddy, smiling so big on those windy, whitecapped days. "I love to see de white 'tings."

Our bartender, Dr. J. "Dis here a traditional rum punch. One part sour, two part sweet, 'tree part strong, four part weak."

The man giving directions past his village. "You must go up so, find de path, stay straight, not to de right or de left, you will find some big stones and den you will reach."

I could have listened all day to Eurlin the boatbuilder, man of the sea. Looking out at the channel, he'd say, "it calm enough out there to ship eggs today." All transactions were "no cash, no splash." Someone in government who annoyed him was "dem scrunters." When he was about to drink a beer he proclaimed, "look out throat, heavy rain comin'." Or speaking about his wife or his double-ender boat, "she sweet like sugah, ya know!"

There were impromptu parties on yachts and local jump ups on the beach. It rained so hard it rained upward, soaking us instantly, wavering in sheets so thick we couldn't see across the street. Then clear and sunny again, everything dripping wet and a rainbow out to sea.

Bequia was baby turtles all paddling faithfully toward the ocean in their tanks at Brother King's turtle sanctuary. It was a prickly hike to the wild north end, sunset at the Whaleboner, snapper at Nando's tiny place in the trees. It was blues all night at the Plantation House until the power went out with a bang. It was the Rasta veggie market, the ferry rides, the lean waterfront stevedores.

Bequia will always be our enchanted island.

Sailors talk about going to Fiddler's Green when they die, and the Greeks hoped for the Fortunate Isles, but I have found my paradise. When my time has come, I don't want endless fiddlers, dancing and tobacco. I don't need mythical gods and heroes.

I want wind in the hills. I want long swells and friendly shores. Give me Bequia.

CONFESSION

EVERY DAY IS A JOURNEY, AND THE JOURNEY ITSELF
IS HOME. –MATSUO BASHO

A t the end of it all, after my wild leap into the unknown, what did I find in those islands? What did
I gain in exchange for that time and life energy I
offered up so recklessly to the cause?

Where to begin? I will forever owe an immense debt of grati-
tude to the Grenadines, for my five seasons as a captain there
profoundly changed me and the trajectory of my life.

I came to the islands at a time when I was unsure of everything. And I was answered in wind and thunder and made whole.
The sea forced the big questions and offered exquisite answers.

Down there, I finally faced directly my various fears, those
boogeymen that had chased me for so long. I found that fear is
an illusion, a trick we insist on playing on ourselves. While I
waited in my first days on that mooring in the lagoon, there was
no end to the storms, sinkings and humiliations that awaited.
But those things were only a mirage. You needed to get amongst
it, to know your adversary, to look the sea monster squarely in
the eye. You needed to get inside its skin and know its thoughts.

Then there was no more monster.

When in doubt, I learned to wait and see, to watch as the universe unfolded a plan better than I could have imagined. I learned to be curious, and as James Stephens says, "Curiosity will conquer fear even more than bravery will."

Even more important, I began to understand that I, that all of us, held a mysterious power beyond what the textbooks might ever have told us. "You are not a drop in the ocean. You are the entire ocean in a drop," Rumi said. That realization, once felt to the very core, changes everything. "Who sees all beings in his own self, and his own self in all beings, loses all fear," says the Upanishad. That was, and continues to be, an absolute game changer.

I still see those fears emerge, and who does not? We are humans, and we will always be a little jumpy about our mortality and the passage of time, about the possibilities of physical harm, of grievous loss and separation. But now I do not fight or flee as my default mode. Now those thoughts and fears are only clouds, drifting across the skies of consciousness. They will go and other thoughts will take their place. They do not tell me what to do. I can choose my response.

And those butterflies before action? I've learned those are the best. They are courage itself, beating against my heart.

These days, those unwelcome thoughts and feelings that once seemed so overwhelming are more like passengers on my boat. They may be loud, insistent, threatening or cajoling, but I know they are simply passengers. My job is to watch after them, sometimes mightily amused by their clamor, and take command. Regardless of their unruliness, I can still steer the ship safely home.

I learned that much of this was in my blood, after all. I could harness the courage of my grandfathers who had fallen a massive spruce or climbed onto an unbroken horse. That courage carried in my DNA helped me do the mighty deeds and the simple ones too. I drew on the empathy of my mother, the nurse, and took from my father his preacher's sense of a great mission, of doing the thing, and his teacher's knack of passing along knowledge and keeping a steady hand even if things might be falling apart beneath you. My dad had shown me at a young age how to fix a go-cart, a motorcycle and old cars, and that tinkering came in mighty handy on boats, too. So thank you, Mom and Dad.

I discovered a calling. I found something I could do with confidence and pride. For the rest of my life, no other work would ever be so true, so close to the bone, so exhausting, so envied and absolutely packed with joy.

I learned about humans, in all our messy, strange and compelling ways. I saw my guests clearly at close quarters in that tropical light, and they saw me. On a boat there is nowhere to hide. All the skills or titles we may have had back home meant not a thing here. The most brilliant of surgeons might be someone you could not turn your back on for a second on a boat. And book learning only went so far. There were other things that mattered most as shipmates: A sense of humor, courtesy, adaptability and a willingness to pitch in.

Some of my clients have stayed great friends. Others have drifted off into life's stream again. Some are gone. Some are now Olympic sailors. We shared a place, a time and discoveries both within and without. I heard their jokes, replaced a tooth and plucked a fishbone from a trachea. I held onto some to console them and others to keep them in line. I found in people a lot to like and not much to dislike; ultimately there was more to empathize with than anything else.

It was all there, the ugly and sublime. I saw starving dogs and misguided boys throwing rocks at them, but I also saw people who made it their life's work to save those dogs. The Why Knot lady would sell her handmade wares and give it all to the island animals. For every ignorant person out there at sea somewhere who had tossed their plastic into the water, willing volunteers would clean it off the beach. For each turtle butchered for food, the saintly Brother King coaxed dozens more young ones back into the sea.

The youthful energy of the island kids, playing in the surf together in harmony, was always a cause for optimism. Our island friends had discovered a simple joy not found back in the headlong pace, sales quotas and earnings reports of the north.

I found that the longer I spent with the sea and its marvelous creatures, the more my own personal madness subsided. My compensatory cravings for danger, discomfort and physical attraction could shift instead toward curiosity, connection and love.

I learned that no matter how exotic the anchorage or how fine the yacht, we make our own happiness. As Robert Pirsig says, "The only Zen you can find on the tops of mountains is the Zen you bring up there." I've been in gorgeous places where people were bitching about broken boat gear and oblivious to the sunset. I've heard a screaming match between a couple on a boat ironically named Tranquilo. I've also been in miserable weather on a broken boat with people who absolutely lit up the place, who laughed and were kind.

That kindness, it seems to me, is everything. Yes, love is all we need. But kindness is the evidence of love. Acts of kindness big and small, gifted to me by complete strangers, were the reason I survived and thrived as a sailboat skipper. I only hope I can continue to pass those kindnesses along all my life.

There was a certain energy to the Grenadines that I have not found anywhere else. It was laid back and peaceful, but also always in motion. It whispered, what will be will be, and what will be will always change. Waves had energy. The tropical sunshine had energy. And people responded to it. It changed their energy and it changed mine for good. If we could all be perfectly at ease but always in motion, like the rest of nature, what a marvelous existence it could be.

In the Grenadines, on boats, I had direct contact with the world in a way I had not found elsewhere. And that is what I really wanted. I had read my Henry David Thoreau, that seeker who was afraid of the sea and found the forest instead:

"I went to the woods (for me, the sea) because I wished to live deliberately, to front only the essential facts of life, and see if I could not learn what it had to teach, and not, when I came to die, to discover that I had not lived. I did not wish to live what was not life, living is so dear; nor did I wish to practice resignation, unless it was quite necessary. I wanted to live deep and suck out all the marrow of life, to live so sturdily and Spartan-like as to put to rout all that was not life, to cut a broad swath and shave close, to drive life into a corner, and reduce it to its lowest terms, and, if it proved to be mean, why then to get the whole and genuine meanness of it, and publish its meanness to the world; or if it were sublime, to know it by experience, and to be able to give a true account of it in my next excursion."

Yes to all of that, and much more.

On boats at sea, I learned the happiness of small routines and simple pleasures and the absurdity of trying to hang onto more than you need. I found the universe would not let you hang on, that the current was too strong, and all you could really do was let go. The wind keeps blowing, the waves continue to roll, and all that energy is our energy, too, after all.

That much I can tell you with absolute certainty: the whole thing is connected. The mystics and the psychonauts have it right. As surely as the moon pulls the tides, our smallest act makes a ripple that crosses oceans and may become a tsunami. John Muir said, "When one tugs at a single thing in nature, he finds it attached to the rest of the world." I know that the fish feels the barb of my hook just as much as I feel it in the flesh of my own hand.

Out in those ever-changing tides, I found that I am a verb, not a noun, and that we are all a process, not a thing. Think about that carefully and it will change your life. That discovery alone was worth the entire price of admission.

One more thing. I learned how important it was to take care of myself. Actors use a wonderful term, The Instrument, for their breathing, voice and movement. They know they must cultivate and protect their instrument, for their art depends on it. For me, the instrument became my body and my senses. I needed them to do my job, to move through the world, to connect with other creatures, to understand, to delight and to share.

This realization hit me very hard one day as I was doing something both physically and psychologically challenging: Helping an old man get into a boat. Sometimes we had a guest who had trouble moving between the sailboat and the tender, and I'd done this before.

But as I looked into this man's eyes, ice blue, something about this moment struck a nerve deep within me. I was holding his body as his thin legs struggled to find his footing. His face was angry, frustrated and ashamed. His young wife waited patiently. This man had everything in his portfolio, and nothing left in those pins. "What shall it profit a man, if he gain the whole world and lose his legs?"

Stay sharp and stay strong, I thought.

And never wait. Do the thing now.

That man didn't know it, but he put me over the edge. I'd grown up with healthy habits, but now I border on the obsessed.

I see my body, not as a temple, but as an antenna, or perhaps a live wire. I want to be able to plug completely into the flow of the universe, and I want to feel that energy as clearly as possible. I want to transmit it along to others.

And I want to act. I believe, as Ernest Hemingway wrote, "The shortest answer is doing the thing." If you are curious, explore now. If you have done wrong, make it right now. If you are fearful, face it now. Never put your life on the layaway plan. That's what that old man's legs taught me.

Since then, boats have put me in touch with people and places far beyond the ordinary. Boats deliver magic, plain and simple.

I could tell you of sailing the Amalfi Coast of Italy, of circumnavigating Vancouver Island, of transiting the Panama Canal. But instead I think of a gnome-like Frenchman I met that very first season in Grenada who helped me jumpstart my boat's dead batteries. His boat was so hideously cobbled together that I snickered to myself to think it might be the ugliest thing I'd ever seen. But, as these islands were also reminding me, understanding is everything.

So I took the time and asked for his story. He was a welder by trade. He had lost his job and then his wife had left him, both in the same week.

"For a while I was sure I'd just kill myself, end it all," he said. "But I was always looking out my window at this big pile of metal. So I started building a boat."

And where many dream and fail, he actually succeeded. In that marvelously mismatched sailboat built of castoff scrap metal, he made it across the Atlantic.

Here his story had a happy ending since he'd met an island girlfriend who loved his steel home. Now the French welder was anchored in one of the prettiest parts of the world, sharing the same views as the billionaires on their megayachts. I was certain the ripe mangos he was peeling for breakfast tasted extra sweet.

Of all the roles I've played in this one mad and precious existence, nothing comes even close to the one called captain.

I love being at the helm, knowing precisely what to do. I love living in real time with immediate risk and reward. I love being in the elements, my animal senses alive. I've never been as certain of anything as when I'm in command of a boat.

On boats, my fumbling, anxious self and I and all the voices in my head finally found a place we belonged.

When I sail, it's sublime. When I wake up on a boat, it's sheer bliss. I took the plunge, made peace with the sea monsters and chased the dream as far as I knew how.

I will take this charmed life as long as it possibly allows.

CONNECTION

A s a sailboat captain, I must trust the quantifiable measures of my trade: atmospheric pressure, fluid dynamics, magnetic pull and the rest.

I believe a good knot will hold, the right course will lead safely home, a marine head under back pressure will explode, and the natural laws can otherwise make or break you anytime.

But I have felt forces reaching past science into magic, like the wind with all its ridiculous tomfoolery. I can't blame seafarers for their superstitious ways.

Out here, I find something beyond belief; a primitive but direct comprehension, a respect and dare I say love for the great mechanisms of the thing, the push and pull, creations and destructions, the fragilities and brutalities at play.

At times I feel it in pure junkie sensation, my body itself as an antenna, on high alert colliding and colluding with it all, feeling the pulses, pains and intensities... Wowwie!

Along the way, in perpetual motion through many miles and adventures big and small, I have developed a devout belief in waving to every boat I see.

The true boat wave should be an open hand raised high above the head. I like to throw it up there with some gusto–it feels good–and leave it up a long moment to show I mean business.

I have exchanged the goodwill gesture with all manner of other craft, sharing that shiver of pleasure in its return. I have waved madly to billionaire yachts and Mayan dugout canoes. I've seen that a dark low craft speeding toward me off a foreign shore makes a far different impression once its occupants break out in friendly waves.

Far out to sea, I've chanced upon another small vessel going the opposite direction, our two tiny dots of matter trading compass points. That hand held up from the other boat as it rose and fell on the wide spaces held a startling force.

I've seen my wife wave back at me across a tropical anchorage, returning back to our own little boat that is home, and felt that particular wave go straight to my heart.

I believe I am obligated to wave, no matter my own state of affairs, and no matter what I think of the size of the other's wake, noise of their engine, cut of their jib or color of their flag.

A waterborne conveyance passes, and now my arm goes up - a reflex of the best kind.

I even believe in waving to the guy who has just landed a massive river-run salmon, with much hooting and hollering, right out of the very place where I've been fishing my heart out all day with no luck at all. Yes, that wave hurt, but I did it anyway.

Not every boat waves back. Some people stare, then look away, without even a wiggle of the fingers or a lift of the chin. This used to make me feel angry and even abandoned. Not anymore!

These days, I believe I know why. I've decided that their waving arms are broken, or maybe only severely sprained, and they just need time to heal.

So in some harbor someday, if you see a sailor waving like a fool, it might be me. Why not? We are all in fragile craft transiting a brilliant, perilous, one-of-a-kind voyage together, no matter our current heading.

So I'll keep waving, and I hope, my friend, my fellow wayfarer, that you will see my hand across the water, and you will wave back at me.

EPIPHANY

AND HE THINKS ONCE MORE OF AN ISLAND MADE
TO HIS MEASURE, OR RATHER, TO THE MEASURE
OF HIS DREAMS. –UMBERTO ECO

L ooking back on it all, I remember one trip with special clarity. Like most of my adventures in those days, it started with the same voice on the phone.

"Looks like we need you up north then, old boy."

The accent was impossible to place; another black sheep of the Caribbean, an intercontinental vagabond with a questionable past, washed up broken on our shores. There had always been trouble in his haunted eyes and trembling hands as he lighted endless Dunhills, in the empty wine bottles collecting beside his elbow late into the evenings and the Svengali grip of his dark tales. And yet there was his absolute kindness to the weakest around him and his soft spot for animals of all kinds, especially the 500-pound swimming pig who followed him everywhere.

I protested that I didn't know anything about the French islands where he wanted to send me.

"No worries, I'll give you a bit of a briefing. You'll be fine, mate."

I packed my seabag yet again, reluctantly kissed my wife goodbye and boarded the ferry, watching our fairy-tale island slide into the distance.

After the lackadaisical green and blue rhythms of small island life, it was novel to be on an airplane and to be dropped into a land of freeways and tall buildings, where I was whisked away immediately in a Mercedes Benz taxi by a driver in crisp white slacks and a polo shirt.

What a thrill to stroll the waterfront of a strange new town after dark. It was warm and there were foreign languages on the wind; smells of coffee, cigarettes and fresh bread.

I looked at the rows of gleaming yachts. The key to one of those boats was in my pocket, and in the morning I would figure out how to point that boat south. These sensations all tugged at me until sleep took over.

In the morning I began a careful inventory of my new command. Everything depended on the many systems doing what they should. I ran the engine, checked the bilge pumps, counted life jackets and looked over the rigging. I checked the things we'd need to be out on charter for two weeks. I began to think about departure: What was the right course out of here without running aground? How would I get away from the dock in this nice boat, in these tight quarters, with that stiff easterly wind now coming off the beam?

The day was getting well along by the time we slipped the lines. The guests yammered away in New York-ese, peppering me with questions, still wearing the clunky shore shoes they refused to remove. They all stood up on deck, eagerly sightseeing while I departed the marina, which made it hard for me to spot the red and green buoys marking the difference between a fun afternoon and making a new shipwreck on these shores.

But we did make it out unscathed, and we did set the sails to enjoy one of life's finer pleasures: A beam reach across flat water in the Caribbean wind and sunshine, the bow of the boat pointed toward the horizon, the sounds of mere wind and water, the sensations of sweet and fluid motion. Even these amped-up Easterners seemed strangely soothed by it all.

But there is always a price to pay, and ours came when we reached our destination, these fetching little islands called Les Saintes. The anchorage was packed with boats and it was late in the day. I picked my way in, chose a spot for the night and instructed the fitter-looking guest to drop the anchor. I was very disappointed when the anchor dragged not once, but four or five times. Night was coming on in that sudden way it does in the tropics, and our boat was still a drifting object that had not connected to the earth.

By now my struggles had become the object of much attention. My passengers fired nervous questions, and many of the other skippers in the bay began to emerge onto their decks and look or point in my direction. Some waved me away, shouting in various languages. I was the scourge of the anchorage, the outcast of the seas, that skipper who drags anchor.

As dark came, I moved the boat once more, went to the bow myself and had a heartfelt chat with that anchor and then dropped it once again. It seemed to hold in tentative fashion.

And then the wind began to blow. All that energy, so lovely earlier in the day, now pushed against my boat and my uncertain anchor, conspiring against me.

Certainly the charter captain has many roles: Navigator, meteorologist, medic, mechanic, storyteller, counselor, chef. The captain calms fears, staves off sunburns and steadies seasick stomachs. A charter captain, late in the evening, hears more interesting stories than a psychiatrist might. Life's tales swirl in a boat's wake, a jumble of emotional flotsam and jetsam, dreams, desires and disappointments.

But the trickiest role is recreating an impossible fantasy. The charter guest has just paid a great deal of money to be bobbing gently in a tranquil bay, sipping a cool drink. Or as one charter brochure reads: "You're all toasty and golden, sailing from one tropical island to another, snorkeling in deliciously clear water, grilling fresh-caught fish, no calls, no bills, no clients."

All wishful thinking and misguided blather, says the charter captain, who would like to have a word or two with that copy-writer who's obviously never served in the trenches.

Nonetheless, it remains the captain's job to reconcile this blissful nonsense with broken boats, leaky heads, constant squalls, murky waters schooled with jellyfish, pushy boat boys, crowded harbors and questionable moorings.

The guest sees an island on the horizon and falls in love. The skipper's squint toward the same island is more world-weary. He knows about the oil leak, and how he will have to redline the poor engine like one might flog a reluctant donkey in order to get to that island which might as well be a mirage.

The charter guest has heard of this fantastic anchorage from another lawyer pal and absolutely wants to go in there. She imagines sunset in a deserted lagoon, the swim ladder down in gin-clear water, a slight breeze tickling the palm trees and her trophy husband's hair.

The captain looks at the high seas and tries to guess how

much the boat will roll at anchor. And he wonders if that disco on shore still plays until three in the morning, competing with the revival tent across the bay at higher and higher decibels. He sees where someone has opened a hatch on the foredeck, and he knows that every wave is putting a little more salt spray onto the unfortunate guest's bed and that he's going to hear about it.

The captain's life looks easy and indulgent enough when floating at anchor under the stars, telling stories over dinner or diving into the lagoon. And no joy compares to setting sail for a new island on a perfect morning, rising over swells, watching the trade winds drive clouds across the sky. There is an unmistakable pride to be making a real and vital living with head and hands, making precise judgments with immediate rewards, letting trivial things fall into the wake, senses alive, riding air and water. What a fine feeling to steer by fingertips, feeling the wind's breath, watching the sea change beneath the bow.

But it can turn in a hurry. And when everything falls apart, those superlatives can ruin you. There is no time clock to punch out and scurry away home. This is your boat, your situation, in a foreign place, in the grip of uncertain weather and mechanical blowouts. Those are the times you earn your keep and find out if you're really cut out for this life.

Right then, in Les Saintes, my duty was anchor watch. With the guests back from dinner ashore and gone to bed, I was alone with the wind and with my bitter anchoring regrets. I wished I'd put out a second anchor. I wished I'd bargained for a mooring ball. Now the mast keened with wind. Great blasts came unrelenting against the boat.

There was another big gust and a ripping sensation. The boat skidded sideways, heading, I knew, for a pack of other boats and then the reef beyond. I jumped to the wheel and fired up the engine. An alert guest burst from below and climbed toward the bow. Much appreciated! Together we would raise the useless anchor, escape these boats and this reef and find somewhere else to hunker for the night. It's not how I was hoping to spend the next few hours, but it could be done.

As I shifted forward, the diesel engine gave a shriek and a shudder, then died. The squall hit at the same moment, a slashing of wind and water, stinging my lips, so much rain I couldn't see. A skipper's nightmare: the boat out of control, pushed by weather into hazards, at night, no sure way it might end.

But wait. I pressed the starter, shouting at the engine, and it fired up. I tried to reverse, and got just enough power to back out of a couple near misses with dimly seen boats.

Through the torrent I could see the doctor and the ad exec were at the bow, bending over the anchor and pulling hard. They'd both seemed primed for a heart attack just climbing aboard earlier today, and I really hoped it didn't happen now.

I heard a clunk as they got the anchor back up.

"DROP. IT. HERE." I shouted into the wind.

The boat swung to and felt like it held.

I blew out a breath of relief. I looked around and there was just barely enough room here for the night, if we could stay put this time.

I dug deep into the locker, untangled a second anchor that looked small enough to be a toy and wrestled it into the dinghy. I coaxed the suddenly reluctant outboard engine for yet another push into the wind. I finally got that backup anchor down.

It was midnight, and my body was sending signals of retreat, fatigue coursing through my forearms, neck and shoulders. My willpower was fading fast.

Just one more chore. I knew why that engine had died. There was undoubtedly one of our lines wrapped around the prop, in this case a stray jib sheet that had likely gone overboard in the excitement. A classic mistake, and as skipper, nobody's fault but mine.

I wouldn't sleep until the wrong was right. I wrapped a head-lamp in a plastic bag, grabbed a galley knife, stripped down to my skin, adjusted my mask and plunged in. Salt water stung the cuts on my hands. Faces leaned over the rail.

"What's he doing down there? Crazy!"

Wind waves splashed over my head. I took two big slow breaths, then four rapid shallow ones, a trick that fools the brain and allowed me to stay down longer. I went under the boat in the heaving dark.

Sure enough. In the thin beam of light, there was that line wound tight around the prop shaft. In a dozen dives, sawing away with a serrated blade, it came away.

The wind dialed down just a notch. The anchors seemed to be keeping us off the rocks. And now my prop was free, just in case.

I rinsed off the salt and dried with a rough towel, all my senses sharp and pulling. Orion and his faithful dog soared overhead, and beyond was the shimmering trail of the Milky Way. I felt the ache of muscle and the sting of wind.

The real thing, cowboy.

Sooner or later, a captain's got to get some sleep. As I waited for the adrenaline to wear off, I let my mind run.

I thought about human effort. With these trips, I'd lived many realities through my guests. Some had worked and waited a lifetime for this. Along the way they'd built up enough habits, afflictions and addictions to quash the experience. They couldn't quite enjoy themselves anymore.

Others had set out to change the world, and now, confronted with a sudden life change, they'd retreated here to a boat, not sure what was next. The newlyweds and the newly divorced. Bankrupt giants of industry. A human wave of time and talent, spent on what? We lived our lives chasing slippery things.

For my part, my body was bone tired from pulling anchor chains, tugging outboards and grinding winches. Viewed objectively, I'd spent all that energy only to shift a floating bit of plastic from one speck on the map to another.

A plane passed against the infinity of stars. No reason I couldn't be on that plane. As anybody; a securities trader, perhaps, one of the new pirates, a hard, unblinking man of the world. Or a humanitarian off to rescue the victims of disaster. A novelist on tour. Or the pilot himself, self-assured and necessary in his cockpit, shrinking the distances, cruising above the ordinary, home in time for dinner.

Other worlds. A small shift of plans at some critical junction, that's all. A nudge in another direction. The tricks of genetics and circumstance. A previous resolve to take things a little more seriously, or perhaps a little less. I questioned my own revisionist history, its outcomes infinitesimal and deductions pointless, a game hardly worth playing.

And how was I spending that dwindling currency, the only true thing we hold, the coinage of time itself? What was my one vital purpose?

On that epic night, I remember taking one more deep breath, standing out there in the elements, floating in space.

All those questions faded to pure sensation.

Tonight, this was plenty.

All I needed was trade winds, sunrise and stars. All that mattered was the next passage to a new place, in time with the tides and the seasons. My clear purpose was in command of this sailboat, of any sailboat, hauling on lines, watching for squalls, seeing flying fish erupt from water more blue than any of my hungriest boat dreams could ever have been.

My duty was here on the water, living my life in growing circles like the frigate birds above, doing my small chores in honest bone and muscle with my fellow creatures everywhere.

Right now, it was enough to have the undiluted pleasure of guiding a ship across the sea, to let my heart rise up to meet the challenge and to feel the sweet, sweet tug of the wind.

UNTITLED

EPILOGUE

"Instructions for living a life.
Pay attention.
Be astonished.
Tell about it."
-Mary Oliver

ACKNOWLEDGEMENT

Everyone I have met in life has taught me something. I am grateful for all the teachers I have had along the way, beginning with my parents and that little boat Dad built and named *Skipper-N-Dad.* Thank you especially to Gartly Curtis, who hauled me across the Pacific as crew and showed me a way of life from which I have never recovered. Gartly, it's all your fault. Thank you to the Caribbean charter manager who hired me sight unseen and took me under his wing. Thank you to all my sailing clients. Thank you to Mother Nature for always putting on a first-class show. Thank you to my beta readers, Jon, Linn, Lily, Sholeh & Mike. And most of all, thank you to my forever muse, the lovely and unstoppable Rebecca, my co-captain on boats, on islands and in life.

ABOUT THE AUTHOR

David Kilmer

The author grew up in seven houses and three countries. As a kid he made a collection of bullets and bomb fragments from the streets of Beirut, Lebanon, and he learned to drive dodging buffalo and giraffe in a Peugot 504 in the game parks of Kenya. After college at Walla Walla University, he worked as a wildland firefighter, EMT, small town reporter, sailing instructor, ski bum and magazine editor. But none of this prepared him for the absolute joy, terror and moment-by-moment purity of being a Caribbean boat captain. David lives in Coeur D'Alene, Idaho, and Barra de Navidad, Mexico and travels at every possible chance. From 2009-2019, David and his co-captain, Rebecca, cruised their 36-foot sailing sloop from Bellingham, Washington, to the Bahamas with stops in 12 countries including Cuba along the route. David is the editor of CdA Magazine and captain of the private yacht Sizzler.

Made in the USA
Coppell, TX
14 February 2023

12796836R00089